AF657402

Ao Naga World-view: A Dialogue

Ao Naga World-view

A Dialogue

Sujata Miri
Karilemla

Indian Council of Philosophical Research
New Delhi

D K PRINTWORLD
Publishers of Indian Traditions

Cataloging in Publication Data — DK

[Courtesy: D.K. Agencies (P) Ltd. <docinfo@dkagencies.com>]

Miri, Sujata.

Ao Naga world-view : a dialogue / Sujata Miri, Karilemla.
p. cm.
ISBN 13: 9788124608081

1. Ao (Indic people) – History. 2. Ao (Indic people) – Social life and customs. 3. Nāgāland (India) – Social life and customs. I. Karilemla, 1978-, joint author. II. Title.

DDC 305.800954165 23

ISBN 13: 978-81-246-0808-1

First published in India, 2015 Print run : 550 copies

© Sujata Miri (b. 1942) and Karilemla (b. 1978)

All rights reserved. No part of this publication may be reproduced or transmitted, except brief quotations, in any form or by any means, electronic or mechanical, including photocopying, recording, or any information storage or retrieval system, without prior written permission of the copyright holder, indicated above, and the publishers.

The contents of this book and the views expressed herein are solely of the authors. The authors of this publication have taken all possible care to ensure that the contents of this publication do not violate any existing copyright or other intellectual property rights of any person(s) or organization(s) in any manner whatsoever. In the event of the authors failing to track any source and if any copyright has been inadvertently infringed, please notify the ICPR and the co-publisher in writing for corrective actions in the subsequent edition.

Published by:
INDIAN COUNCIL OF PHILOSOPHICAL RESEARCH
Darshan Bhawan, 36 Tughlakabad Institutional Area
Mehrauli Badarpur Road, New Delhi - 110 062

and

D.K. PRINTWORLD (P) LTD.
Regd. Office: "Vedaśrī", F-395, Sudarshan Park
(Metro Station: Ramesh Nagar), New Delhi – 110 015
Phones: (011) 2545 3975, 2546 6019; *Fax*: (011) 2546 5926
e-mail: indology@dkprintworld.com
Website: www.dkprintworld.com

Printed by : D.K. Printworld (P) Ltd. New Delhi

Dedicated to

Meyawati Walling and *Yabangchila Imchen*

Preface

This work is the culmination of the research undertaken by us over a long period of time. It took final shape after the Indian Council of Philosophical Research, New Delhi made a token grant under the aeigis of the project entitled "World-view of Tribes of Northeast India" in 2008-10, which enabled us to fund a number of workshops with tribal elders. Dr Prasenjit Biswas the co-ordinator of the project, Prof. Vanlalnghak, Prof. G Mishra and Prof. Mrinal Miri, members of the Advisory Committee, facilitated our work for which we acknowledge with gratitutde their help and guidance.

The book consists of recorded conversations about traditional Ao practices, beliefs about the human condition, the ethical grounding of human life, the dividing line between life and death, and about their institutions for educating the young and dispensing justice.

The purpose of the conversation is two-fold: (1) to secure an authentic articulation of the traditional Ao world through a dialogue between different Ao voices (an aim pursued very differently from the Anthropologist's participant observation), and (2) clearing the ground for the reflection on philosophical insights thrown up in the process of this articulation. The insights will be obvious to the sympathetic and discerning reader; the reflection is left to those who will read the book with serious philosophical interest.

The conversation is free flowing and continuous – only very gently guided by the Visitor, a retired University Professor of

Philosophy. There is, therefore, no sharp division of the book into distinct chapters. The "chapterization" however very roughly follows thematic distinctions and the chronological order of the original.

The book also includes a few paintings by Sujata Miri in the hope that they might add a different dimension to our understanding of Ao narratives. A note about the paintings is added at page ix.

Prof. Temsula Ao a noted personality of the North-East and a valuable friend actively participated in one of our sessions with the Ao elders. We are immeasurably grateful to her for her time and contribution. We owe special thanks to Dr Sashinungla Ao of the Department of Philosophy, Jadhavpur University, who gave us immense help in making our understanding of Ao heritage more systematic and focused. Dr C.J. Thomas, Deputy Director NERC, ICSSR, Shillong was always with us in planning, hospitality and recording of our meets. His cooperation was invaluable. So also the assistance provided by Abhishek Kumar, a doctoral research student of Delhi Universty, who put up with us through a long period of trial and error in shaping the manuscript. While the list of elders who form the backbone of the dialogue is attached in the Appendix, we would like to put on record our special gratitude to Mr Lipoktsungba Aier and Mr Samatoshi Walling for their guidance in locating and introducing us to the elders.

Sujata Miri
Karilemla

A Note on the Paintings

THE PAINTINGS included in the book are part of a large corpus of paintings by Sujata Miri. Some of them are taken from her book, *A Book of Paintings on Themes from the Northeast* (2005). The majority of her paintings explore through the medium of painting her own insight into the world of the tribes of India's north-east. They are, in a way, her own particular mode of articulating the imagination embedded in the communities' inherited narratives, tales, legends and songs. They should not therefore be taken as attempts to represent the actual products of the imagination of the communities. There is, however, one thing that is present both in these paintings and in the "tribal" (for want of a better word) imagination which may be described as the expression of human emotions in natural objects that are not human. But that is only natural: it is impossible to tell stories about deep mutually binding emotional, ethical and spiritual ties between humans and things that are not human, without attributing to the latter powers of articulation peculiar to humans. This is, as it were, the inescapable predicament of the human imagination – what may be called the human-centric predicament. But this must not lead to the view that the tribal imagination humanizes the non-human world. Quite the contrary, for the tribesman the non-human world is a perpetual reminder of an other who is also profoundly akin to himself.

Contents

Introduction

THE TEXT consists of conversations on various aspects of Ao history and culture among members of the Ao community. The participants consist of persons who are regarded as "elders" of the community, a college teacher, a student, a retired primary school teacher, persons who have received modern education and are respected members of the community, and "the Visitor" who is the lone "outsider". Most of the elders spoke no language other than Ao, although they might have had some familiarity with languages of neighbouring communities. The conversation therefore took place in Ao. The Visitor had the benefit of translations both ways by the English-speaking participants. The conversation is free-flowing and only very gently guided and lightly coordinated by the "Visitor". The language is emphatically ordinary, totally devoid of any academic or disciplinary orientation. Another significant aspect of the conversation is that it is among complete equals: while there is well-deserved deference to the views of the elders, differences are accepted as natural and countered with seriousness without any obvious claims to finality. It is therefore very different from conversations within the normal framework of anthropological investigation. It is something of the community's non-reductive look at the mirror image of its own life.

Freedom from disciplinary control also means freedom from philosophical intrusions – with its very broad meaning. But there are many things said during the conversation which can serve as telling reminders to philosophers in precisely the sense in which Wittgenstein talked about the philosophical importance of assembling reminders.

In this Introduction I shall touch upon aspects of the conversation which the philosopher might find interesting.

Origin and History

The talking session begins with stories of origin. It is interesting that Aos consider what might be called "historical" speculation about their place of origin and migration from there to what came to be Ao country as irrelevant to the understanding of their culture, and even disrespectful to Ao heritage. Tako Jamir's story is generally accepted:

> A man from Changki village named Ajangtoi expressed the view that Aos did not emerge from the six rocks in Chungliyimti but belonged to the Mongolian race and must have migrated from somewhere. On hearing this, a heavy penalty was imposed on him by the community.

The striking image of "bursting forth" from six rocks is deeply embedded in the collective consciousness of the Aos. This consciousness has a cognitive strength enhanced by an emotional commitment that is largely definitive of Ao identity itself. One would therefore need to think about issues such as possible externality of "history" to a community's sense of identity, the connection between authenticity of mythical "memory" with its ramifications in the complex network of meanings in the body of Ao imaginings and cognitive enterprises and articulation of identity itself. Such an articulation of identity must be distinguished from identity derived from a "memory" – mythical or otherwise – imposed upon a community by external agencies through political and cultural domination: colonial exploitation, religious coercion and so on. Authenticity here is internally connected with an unfailing sense of autonomy.

Songs

It is pertinent here also to reflect on the importance of songs as a binding force of the culture. The text has a large number of songs, which, in English translation, appear soulless. But in the original they have a powerful emotional content and the images have deep multiple resonances. As frequently asserted during the conversation a song – traditionally received – settles a point about life and culture. Product of collective imagination, songs come down from generation to generation and have an objectivity free from deviations through private manipulation. In the words of several of the "elders" songs owned by the community "validate" the culture and ensure its continuity. The emotions embodied in the songs also evoke a strong sense of oneness with the culture.[1]

Rituals

As in all communities rituals are an important part of Ao cultural and religious life. Unlike modern societies, the secular/sacred distinction does not exist for the traditional Ao; also religion is embedded in the culture – thus the culture/religion distinction is also spurious. But rituals which are connected with crucial events of human life have a very special status. They must be performed with meticulous correctness, and strict standards of purity must be observed.

> I would like to inform everybody that they would consult the sangmongtsü (soothsayer) as to whom to choose to perform the ritual in order to ask God's healing of sickness and also for his blessings. Once a person is chosen he makes himself physically clean, will not eat anything even in his children's house. This is how they maintained purity in order to perform rituals. It is considered more important than animal offering. – Merazulu Longchar, 39

---

1 In modern times the national anthems of a country are supposed to serve the same purpose.

Rituals ensure temporal continuity between the past, present and the future; it is, therefore crucial that they themselves have the character of atemporality – a sense of transcendence of time and temporal contingencies.

Man and Animals

In Ao thought there is a clear divide between man and animals:

> In the beginning, god made two types of *meimchir*: One is known as human beings, who have a social and a cultural life, and the other is known as animals that do not have a society. To be truthful and to attain salvation was the highest goal of human life. – Korakaba Jamir, 51

Also man has language in which to communicate with one another; animals do not.

> Animals and plants cannot communicate with others but humans can. This is one of the reasons why they thought that it is better to be born in human form than as animals and plants. – Bendangsashi Longchar, 53

Society, culture and language are inseparably linked; and it is language that makes the distinction between true and false possible. It may be philosophically extremely instructive to reflect on the link between society, culture, language and truthfulness being the highest goal of human life.

The Mind

The following rather apologetic statement is revealing:

> Ao vocabulary is very poor. We don't have a separate word for mind. If we wish to say that "your mind is not working", we simply say "your brain is not working". In our language the word *tekolok* (brain) is used for mind.
>
> – Merazulu Longchar, 53

It is well known that the idea of the mind as an entity totally distinct from and separate from the body is a legacy of Western philosophical thought. That the Ao elder has to be apologetic about there not being a separate word in Ao language for "mind" as distinct from the word that refers to the brain is a clear indication of a cultural domination – subtle enough not to be seen as domination by the "victim" – that I mentioned a little earlier. There are traditions of thought that have treated the mind as part of the body – as even a bodily "instrument" used for purposes specific to humans. Perhaps Ao traditional thought here indicates a philosophical insight the enormous significance of which is being spelt out only in very recent philosophical debates – debates straddling the disciplines of psychology, physiology (brain research) and philosophy. One other very startling thought about the relationship between the brain (mind) and the heart is: "Brain and heart are like siblings"(Guru Sademmeren Longkumer, 52). The philosophical significance of this metaphor should not be lost on anybody who is half way familiar with the debate about emotions and their place in our cognitive enterprise.

Tiya

One of the most fascinating concepts in traditional Ao thought is the concept of *tiya*. Every person inherits a *tiya*:

> When a person is born on this earth, God gives him *tiya*. So, he has to live his life according to his *tiya*. Whatever *tiya* he has, is his share from God. – Guru Sademmeren Longkumer, 60

The *tiya* of a person shapes the general style of his life, the way he/she conducts himself/herself in life, but it also determines whether a person will or will not prosper in life. *Tiya* is similar to luck (some persons are born lucky or born unlucky), but it is not luck. A run of luck or a run of bad luck is something that might happen to a person, and although it might impact his life greatly, it is something that is considered to be outside, external to, the person. *Tiya* is internal to the person and it shapes the person's general demeanour in life; while it is inherited, the good or bad deeds of the person's ancestors might have something to do with its quality.

> If I am truthful, my children will have good *tiya* and if I am untruthful they will have bad *tiya* because it is God who gives *tiya* to everyone. Yes my *tiya* proves the good or bad deeds of my parents and my grandparents. Suppose, my parents lived a very good life on earth and they were truthful. Then their good deeds will make my *tiya* a good one.
>
> – Merazulu Longchar and Guru Sademmeren Longkumer, 62

A person cannot change his/her *tiya* except with very rare divine intervention. However:

> We can only improve our *tiya* if we live a truthful life. Only the truthful ones receive blessings not the untruthful ones. The Aos in the ancient days, lived a very truthful life, Truth was above all for them. – Kikasangla Imchen, 64

So even divine intervention is not arbitrary – it is morally inspired.

No two persons in the world are completely alike because each person's *tiya* is unique to him/her. It not only shapes the quality of his/her life; it gives the unique identity that each person is endowed with. The uniqueness of each person is a fact of life and it is his or her *tiya* that ensures this uniqueness.

> We may have the same body size and build but everyone possesses his own distinct *tiya* that's how we identify ourselves. – Merazulu Longchar, 61

There is, as it were, *tiya* beyond nature and nurture beyond heredity and environment. The concept of *tiya* is thus expected to make a variety of things crucial to the understanding of the human condition clear to us: why some people are prosperous and others not in spite of honest efforts made by the latter; why each person has a stable demeanour and style of life; why each person has a unique identity and why it is moral transformation (change from falsehood to truthfulness) that can change poverty into prosperity. (Both "poverty" and "prosperity" must be understood in a much larger – if you like spiritual sense – than normally.) Whether the concept can withstand the weight of this multiplicity of tasks is another matter, it is therefore a suitable subject for philosophical reflection.

Life and Death

Death is passage – a passage from the life here to life in the world of the ancestors. The body of the person dies and decays, but another – subtler body – which had inhabited this body leaves and proceeds as though in sleep towards the land of the dead. This subtle body is also referred to nowadays as the "soul".

> . . . all the souls of dead people go downward to a world underground where they start a new life. Some other people believe that Diphu *tenem* a mountain beyond the Wokha hills is the land of the dead. It is said that before climbing mount Diphu, the dead wash themselves in a stream called *Longritsü* (stream of bitterness). As soon as they have washed themselves their earthly shapes are transformed into a pale and thin form. So, they weep bitterly knowing that they are dead and they feel nostalgic for the loved ones left behind on earth. Half way from the Longritsü to Diphu *tenem* they are greeted by the souls of the dead people who wait for them. There is a herb on the bank of the Longritsü River called Molunglem Süngo. It is said that once we pluck and smear that *süngo* on our hands all bitter regrets turn into gladness after which the soul gladly enters the Diphu Lima (the land of the dead).

Some of the striking beliefs about life in the land of the dead are:

(i) it is marked by the cheer of festivities and untrammeled happiness ("after death, the souls of the dead live together in Asüyim (the land of the dead) where there are festivities throughout. A story: A dead man's soul had asked his wife to send him his *arong* that he kept at the bottom of his cane basket. And the *arong* did come to him. There are songs that validate the story");

(ii) the dead kins are reunited and resume their earthly relationships;

(iii) life in the land of the dead is stable compared to earthly life which is nothing but a temporary passage;

(iv) communication between the dead and the living is possible, but the dead are never reborn in the land of the living;

(v) the dead – ancestors – do not control life on earth, but there is a benign concern for the troubled life on earth; and

(vi) although Aos now do talk about separation in the land of the dead between "heaven and hell", a voice of authority says,

> Here I beg to differ. Good and bad places such as heaven and hell we have started talking about only after conversion to Christianity. Earlier we only talked about Asüyim or the Land of the dead.

As in most religious traditions, death, for the Aos, does not mark the end of existence. It is, for them, a passage into another very similar form of existence, the one important difference being that life after death is stable, happy and devoid of the unfortunate contingencies of "life on earth". Also, therefore, death is not the end of experience and the end of all kinds of worlds; on the contrary, death is a very special kind of experience – the experience of the transformation of the earthly body into a subtler, transparent body.

An important implication of the relationship between the dead and the living is that the division of time into the past, the present and the future is very differently conceived: the past is, as it were, co-extensive with present and the future – the dead are forever there co-present with the present and the future will similarly be co-present with the present and the past. The community's permanence is thus ensured in its own view of life and the world.

Justice, Objectivity and Fairness

The village council which is largely democratic is responsible for the general administration of the village, and also for settling disputes of various kinds. Fairness and objectivity are inalienable aspects of the system of justice. A dispute within the community that is important enough for the life of the community is taken up for settlement by the council; if the council is unable to resolve it, the matter is referred to the Putuait (retired members of the council); if either of the parties rejects the decision of the Putuait, the entire village must assemble to give the final verdict. It is difficult to imagine a fairer system of administering justice (Merazulu Longchar, 43). Justice must also be seen as totally free from favour shown to either party. If in a particular dispute, it becomes impossible for the administrator of justice to determine the truth or falsehood of the versions presented by the opposing parties, the matter then is taken out of the sphere of human adjudication. One method is to make both parties eat a little soil – the one who becomes sick is proven to be the culprit.

> The village council would give six days' time to the parties after they eat soil. If anything bad happened to either of the parties, that party or person was considered to be the wrongdoer. – Guru Sademmeren Longkumer, 46

Stranger and Friend

A stranger is someone who is not a member of the village community. The Ao word for it is *bendanger*. It is taboo to call a fellow member of the village community *bendanger*. (The modern practice of living among strangers in an urban community must therefore be almost unintelligible to the traditional Ao.) A *bendanger* is looked upon with suspicion, but is not necessarily unwelcome.

> Strangers such as you who come to the village with good intentions are welcome. For it is possible that he may turn out to be your *temba*, meaning best of friends. – Tareptsüba, 127

One can become close friends with a stranger. A stranger who has been allowed to live in the community, and has done very commendable work for the well-being of the community may even be honoured with the title "Nokinketer". "Walunir" and "Nokinketer" are titles with which exceptional persons are honoured.

> Walunir is a person who is ever prepared to sacrifice his life for the people in war and also gives feasts to the villagers by killing *mithuns* while a Nokinketer sacrifices his life for the people in war but does not kill *mithuns* to give feasts to the villagers. A count of *mithun* heads shows how hard working a Walunir was. A Nokinketer is only a warrior but a Walunir is an all-rounder. However both are praiseworthy. The village folk will compose songs for both of them in praise of their good deeds. Nokinketer songs will speak about his valorous actions, sacrifices and how many heads he has brought home, etc. Walunir songs will speak about how many *mithuns* he killed for feasting his villagers, his leadership quality, his sacrifices in the battlefield, etc. – Merazulu Longchar, 133

Temba (friendship) with a member of the same village community, or a member of another village community or even a total *bendanger* includes the obligation to observe a period of mourning and perform the usual rites in honour of the dead friend.

The Institution of Arju

Arju is one of the most ancient ("The institution of *arju* was there since our Chungliyimti times") and fascinating institutions of the Aos. It is the institution through which the traditions of the community – its life-skills, values and the subtly differentiated rules of conduct are handed down to the new generations. Every male child from the age of 11-17, must be a member of the *arju* and receive training from their elders in the *arju*. Primary among the skills taught are the skills of warfare and physical protection of the community; but music, particularly singing that is so closely linked to the history of the community is an important part of the training. Agriculture is another crucial area of training. The guiding values or virtues of *arju* training are obedience, humility, patience, courage and friendship. Thus one might justifiably suggest that these virtues constitute the core and the basis of Ao moral experience. All crucial activities constituting Ao life must be permeated by the practice of these virtues. *Arju* training thus is a complete system of education whose aim was to equip the young with resources to lead a fulfilling community life guided by the ethical principles tested through generations of practices that make up the life of the community. Value education for the Aos was not a separate and independent system of training, it was necessarily embedded in all *arju* activities. Modern thinking about education has much to learn from the Ao ideas of educating its young.

The Break with Tradition

At many places in the conversation there are voices, if subdued, of distress at the irreversible changes that are taking place in Ao society – changes engineered by powerful forces which the traditional resources of the community do not seem able effectively to confront. The forces are mainly two: (1) the compulsions of fitting into a modern political, economic and social ethos dominated, however imperceptibly, by a globally accepted liberal, individualistic frame, and (2) the totally unequal challenge to traditional faith posed by a "world" religion. The response to these two, not entirely unrelated, challenges, has been varied ranging from a desire to opt out of the prevailing system altogether, acceptance of the unqualified superiority of the "world" faith and reduction of the old into a cultural residue, bold and forlorn attempts at clinging to the old, desire for a dialogue between the old and the new, and the "irresistible" pull of the new economic political ethos. Each of these responses needs reflective clarity that is necessary for an authentic articulation of Ao self-awareness. And it is here that the role of philosophy is crucial.

There are many other things in these conversations that might catch the reader's reflective attention and interest. What hopefully I have done is to give just an inkling of the valuable ideas that inform the traditional life and practices of the Aos.

Sujata Miri

Ao Naga World-view: A Dialougue

I

Origin and History

Visitor: Respected elders, fellow teachers and students, I am so grateful that you have given me the opportunity to sit with you all and learn about the world-view of the ancient Aos. My purpose is to collect information about them and arrange it in such a way that readers can get a general idea of what the ancestors thought about life.

Merazulu Longchar: We too are very grateful that persons of repute visit us along with our young fellow Aos. You ask and we will answer what we know. In the process we will also learn from you.

Guru Sademmeren Longkumer: Wait, before we start let me say at the outset that we are grateful to our Almighty God for giving us this opportunity.

Tekatia Imchen: We must not forget that it is God who, after creating the world, made human beings, animals and plants to brighten it up. Man emerged out of the earth.

Visitor: I have met many Naga elders in my travels and I am very confused about the use of the word "Naga". There are so many communities who are referred to as Nagas. There are Manipuri Nagas, Sema Nagas and so on. Please tell us specifically about your community that is known as Aos.

Student: The word *naga* is shrouded in mystery. The general opinion is that it is a name given by the non-*naga*s. In their use it signifies the "naked people". Some senior members of my community informed me that the term *naga* refers to a group of people with pierced ears.

Nungshimangyang Longchar: Once upon a time, human beings were nomads; they wandered from place to place. They say that the "Nagas" came along with the present Manipuri people. There are sixteen *Naga* tribes in what is now Nagaland and the Ao is one of them.

Teacher: The Aos are one of the major tribes of the *Naga*s largely found on the high hills of the Mokokchung district of Nagaland. Their language belongs to the Tibeto-Burman family of languages. The Ao territory is divided into six ranges and named thus: Langpangkong range, Asetkong range, Ongpangkong range, Changkikong range, Japukong range and Tsurangkong range.

Student: Each *Naga* tribe has a language of its own. The Aos too have a distinct language called Ao language. In this language, there are three distinct dialects, Chungli, Mongsen and Changki. Interestingly, Chungli dialect has become the standard Ao language.

Teacher: As the respected elders are well aware, the Aos have no written literature. They have a very rich tradition of oral literature, some of which has now been put down in writing. An oral tradition is naturally dependent totally on memory. Generations of learned elders have passed on their remembered living tradition to succeeding generations. We wish to tap your memory resources to get some light on your ancient ways. This is the primary purpose of this exercise.

The Crossing of the River

Guru Sademmeren Longkumer: We did have a script. During Ongputu (the Ong era), it is said, the Aos had a written script and they preserved the script on an animal hide. One day, a dog snatched the hide which was hung on the wall and ate it. That is how the Aos lost their script. In Chungliyimti the Aos lived for several generations. Here all the social norms, rites and rituals, rules and regulations of village administration were formulated.

It is said that the Aos (both the Chungli and Mongsen

speakers) settled down in Chungliyimti and lived there for several generations. As the population increased, they moved to Aonglenden; they came along the Dikhu River and crossed it by the *arapu* (cane bridge). After they crossed the river they cut off the cane bridge and left the rest of the group who could not cross the cane bridge at the other end. Therefore, those who came crossing the *arapu* were given the name, Aoer (the gone) by the other group, and those who were left behind on the other side were called Müraao (ones who did not come) or Sangtemer, by the Aoer group.

Arenjenba Ozukum: As mentioned by my friend, the Aos and the Sangtemer began their journey together.

Visitor: Who were the Sangtemers?

Merazulu Longchar: The ones who could not cross the river were abandoned and they remained on that side of the river. Therefore, the Aos called them Müraao, or the ones who did not come. Now they are known as Sangtemers. It is the Sangtemer or the Müraao who gave the name Aoer to the ones who crossed the river.

Tako Jamir: Let me explain. After our forefathers lived for a few epochs in Chungliyimti (the first Ao settlement), they wandered from place to place, and reached a river called Tsüla. They made a cane bridge in order to cross the river. After they crossed the river, they cut off the cane bridge thinking that all the people have crossed and reached the same side of the river. The group who crossed the river was called Aoer or the gone ones. The group who were left behind was called the Müraao. This is how the Ao tribe got its name.

Visitor: Is it possible that the group was already known as Aos before they settled down on the fertile land? Or did they, as you suggest, get their name after reaching the land?

Arenjenba Ozukum: They came as any other human beings, with no name or identity as such; only when they cut the other group off from the cane bridge, that the Müraao who could not cross the river gave the name Aoer to them.

Merazulu Longchar: The group had no identity when they came searching for land, only when the Aos cut the others off the cane bridge, these others who were left behind considered themselves very fortunate and came to be known as Sangtemers which means "we are better off". Presently, they are known by this name. The Aos however called them Müraao (ones who did not come). So we may say that both the groups got their identity from each other.

Satiba Jamir: So, the name "Ao" was the gift of the group who were left behind and the Müraao got their name from the group that went away or the gone ones, i.e. the Aoer. They wandered and came as a group there was no head count of how many people actually came.

Visitor: Some of the people we spoke to prefer the name Sangtemer to Müraao.

Student: A person from Süngratsü village told me that the Müraao who were not able to cross the bridge, said to the Aoer, "you have left us and gone but we are more privileged and far better off than you". The name Sangtemer signifies this sentiment.

Tako Jamir: We have a different meaning for the word "Sangtem" in Chungli dialect. Let me illustrate; think of the sound "oh" as it is uttered spontaneously in reaction to something, and compare it with when we say "oh . . . oh . . . oh . . oh" raising our voice, as we utter each 'oh' in a crescendo freely and for long. The latter is what we mean by Sangtemaoang, i.e. go freely and for long.

P. Ato. Jamir: Here let me add one clarification. We are talking only about the Sangtemers. But we must remember some other groups, who came to be known as Chang, Phom and Sangtem, were all known as Müraao. I am referring here to the groups who were left behind. Later on, this group also dispersed and got their different tribe names like Chang, Phom and Sangtem. But generally they were all referred to as Müraao.

Student: You elders are telling us that the use of both the terms Sangtemer and Müraao are correct. Both mark the identity of the same tribe, although their meanings are different.

Teacher: However, it is more appropriate to use the word Müraao than the Sangtemer according to Ao tradition; though we must concede that the notion of Sangtemer expresses truly their feelings – they were happy to be on their own with the resources that were left behind by the Aoer.

Visitor: So, they were happier because of the land they got. The relationship between the Aos and the others takes its root here. Can I say that initially, to start with, the Aos and the Sangtemers were the only two groups?

Teacher: No, originally they were not separate groups. They came as one group with no separate identity as such. But when the cane bridge was cut off by the other group they were divided into two groups. So, the Aos got their name from the ones who were left behind and the Müraao or Sangtemers got their name from the Aos, i.e. the gone ones. It is better to use the word Müraao than Sangtemer because there were other tribes like Chang, Phom and Yimchunger who were also in that group.

Visitor: Since they were in search for more land for themselves, accommodating the others was not desired by them; accordingly they cut off the cane bridge?

Tako Jamir: Last year, the elders from Langpangkong range like Mongsenyimti, Yaongyimsen, Akhoya and Chuchuyimlang have pondered seriously over this question. Some people thought that they must have cut off the cane bridge because of rivalry or misunderstanding, as in relationships of couples. Two villagers in this meeting gave the evidence that the cane bridge was cut off thinking all must have crossed the river.

Unfortunately, there were some people who were left behind but it was not done intentionally. Anyway whoever crossed the river came and settled in Ungma Aonglenden. There were songs sung during the settlement, such as the one I am going to sing for you now.

Oh! Longterokkhu poker
Chungliyimti kongnungi harütemangnanager
Chungliyimti aso asem pezü sanger
Chungliyimti toktsüokoni
Tzüla tzüdi ar apu laka nongjen nonokoni
Tongpa langpa henchen tonokoni,
Aonglenden mesemoko
Aonglenden ali temapangnung
Rongpang akhi mesemoko
Tsüngi ka nung ano tera soli
Soyim lima chatetoko.

English translation:

After we burst out from the six stones
On the hill top of Chungliyimti
People of Chungliyimti lived here for three or four epochs
Then they left Chungliyimti
After we lay the cane bridge, many people crossed over
We settled in Aonglenden.
On the hill top of Aonglenden
We have built our home
In a day, ten women gave birth to ten sons
We named the place Soyim land.

Tako Jamir: The song describes how they laid the cane bridge and crossed the Tzüla River. After they came they settled in Aonglenden. They believed that the land of Aonglenden was fertile. Therefore, they made their home there. In one night, ten women gave birth to ten sons that is why they named the place "Soyim".

Teacher: There are two versions of the story. Some people thought that they have left behind the other group intentionally. Some thought that everyone had crossed the river and no one was left behind, and having made sure of that, they cut off the bridge.

Visitor: What was the necessity of cutting off the bridge?

Tako Jamir: We must remember that they were in constant warfare with their enemies; always alert and afraid of them. So, thinking that all must have crossed the river, they quickly cut off the cane bridge. Many people approve of this version.

Nungshimangyang Longchar: In the group, probably there were people who were not so strong physically. So, they might have lagged behind and come late. The earlier party must have thought that everyone had reached and crossed the river; therefore they cut off the bridge.

Teacher: The group was anxious to move forward in their search for fertile land. Thinking all must have crossed the river, they cut off the cane bridge. Their action was not the result of suspicion, greed, or dispute over land.

Visitor: The word Sangtemer now makes sense to me. As you have explained they, the Aoer, did not think ill of the people they left behind. Neither did the Sangtemer think any worse of them.

Tako Jamir: Rather the people who were left behind considered themselves very fortunate. Müraao are the group who were left behind. "Sangtemer" also indicates that the Müraao told the Ao to go freely. The term "Sangtemer" also means a wish, wishing the Aos well. It could be used to mean, "I wish you well". This version appears to be the best. We called other tribes like Chang, Yimchunger, Phom and Sangtemer as Müraao. When the Sangtem tribe writes their history, they will perhaps explain the meaning of Sangtemer in their own way. What we have discussed just now is the Aos version.

Student: We were advised to use the term Sangtem and not Sangtemer.

Teacher: But we have to find out whether this Sangtem stands for the same Sangtem or the Sangtemsangtema.

Visitor: Are you very sure that there are no records of existing tension, conflict or enmity amongst the two groups that lead to their separation? Historically, there could have been some tension?

Merazulu Longchar: There was no tension and conflict amongst them as such. That is the most accepted version. But we have to admit the possibility of a certain element of greed and cunningness in our ancestors. They wanted to possess more land and did not want to share their land with the other group. Therefore, they might have cut them off.

Guru Sademmeren Longkumer: Yes, there were conflicts over the land because people wanted more and more land for cultivation. Once they occupied the land, they did not allow the others to enter the territory.

Visitor: Each community has its own memory of its past. Harmony, fellow feeling and respect for the spiritual, as well as the struggle to maintain its sovereignty on its land are part of the memory of the tribe and we must take that seriously. Going a little further, let me ask a simple question: were any of the groups who split, hostile to the Aos?

Wars

Tako Jamir: During our forefathers' time, we have a history of warfare. There was warfare amongst the Aos, between villages, with Phom, Mechunger (the present Chang tribe), and with Tzüner (Lotha tribe). The Longkhum villagers fought with Tzüner when they were attacked by the latter. Tzüner were not allowed to enter the heart of the Ao territory. In Longkhum village, people were named after this battle called Tongpangnokdang, "The one who defends against the aggressor". In my village, a woman is named Sangtemtangla simply because warriors of her village had chopped off the head of a Sangtemer! Then again, Longra village which belongs to Mechunger tribe now known as Chang have a history of warfare with my villagers. Our forefathers had fought with Litem, Longra, Noksen, they are all known now as the Chang tribe.

Imtinochet Jamir: When the Ao ancestors lived in Chungliyimti, they fought with the Oronger and Lisüer. I am not sure whether they belong to Sangtem or Mechunger tribe. There is a song sung during the so-called Medemsanger Putu (name of an era) which mentions this warfare.

Teacher: You are telling us about the wars between the Aos and others but you are silent about what caused the wars. There must have been some reason why they fought. To know the reason is also very important.

Pangchenmeren: When the Aos settled and started living in Chungliyimti, their enemies were Oronger and Lisüer. Later on, when they migrated, spread and settled in different parts of the Ao territory every village had enmity with their surrounding neighbours. The Longkhum villagers fought with the Lothas because they shared a boundary with Lothas. Some fought with the Sangtemer, some with Phom tribe, etc. mostly with the neighbouring tribes and villages.

Arsashi Jamir: The Oronger and Lisüer are the tribes who were not settled in Chungliyimti. In fact, there are also accounts of fights between the Chungli and Mongsen speakers both members of the Ao group living together in Chungliyimti itself!

Teacher: There is no specific evidence to suggest that some groups were already living there when they came and settled in Chungliyimti for them to have waged war against them. After they lived for a few decades in Chungliyimti, they migrated to different parts of Ao territory and then the wars followed. May be the wars were against the Müraao group. We are not sure.

Student: Dear sirs, can we conclude from the discussion so far that the first war the Aos ancestor fought with others was with the Oronger and Lisüer. Later, when they migrated to different parts of Ao territory, they fought with their neighbouring villages and tribes?

Visitor: Sorry to intervene. What about the people of the plains, the neighbouring Assamese?

Tako Jamir: I come from Langpangkong range and we have a story about war with the Tsümar or the people of the plains.

Imtinochet Jamir: I have not heard of any war with the plains' people.

Tako Jamir: I am talking about those of us who come from the Langpangkong range, and we do have a story about war with Tsümar. Our ancestors came to know the Tsümar's nature very well. If for instance, I killed a Tsümar's brother, Tsümar does not have the sense of taking revenge by killing my brother. Our ancestors thought that strangely enough Tsümars did not have any sense of taking revenge for the killing of parents and siblings. There are songs to validate this. Here the narrator is telling the Tsümar:

Shizungmetsü ashitor
Narotor arongma
Oh ana medema esü henlaki
Tsümarla abhila amangmeyim
Rabiota

English translation:

In terms of wealth, you are the richest
Come, we shall fight
Though we share the same boundary and drink the water from the same source.

Tsümar never bothers to take revenge for their parents and people.
You are the other.

Our ancestors fought with Tsümars and sang this song for them. The Aos have a strong sense of patriotism and would sacrifice their lives for their own loved ones and for their people. Impressed with this trait of the Aos, the Ahom king called Pangjunglemba from one of our villages and gifted him with a pair of shoes made of metal and made peace with him in order to stop the war with the Aos. So, we have fought with Tsümars. The tension ceased only after the peace agreement.

The Warrior's Spirit

Imtinochet Jamir: We had lots of misunderstanding with the Tsümars yet we have never fought as fiercely with them as we fought with other tribes and did not take their heads as trophies.

Teacher: They were not particularly interested in taking a Tsümar's head as a trophy. The song that was sung just now was expressive of their contempt of Tsümars. "Tsümar does not have the warrior's spirit in them. Even if something happened to their mother or parents they will not go and take revenge. They will not go, mourn, and protect their own parents and siblings." The Ao ancestors looked down on them, their way of living and their nature, so they thought there was no point in waging war with them and bringing their heads as trophies.

Student: Aos made alliance with the Assamese for only trade and commerce and not to own and possess their land.

Tako Jamir: The people from Changkikong range used to go to Naganijan for trading purposes. People from Langpangkong range used to go to Amguri.

Imtinochet Jamir: People from Langpangkong range used to trade in Dokhuka and people from Asetkong, Ongpangkong and Changkikong ranges traded in Saringrongpang. In olden days, there were two trading and business centres, between the Aos and the Assamese, i.e. Saringrongpang and Dokhuka.

Tako Jamir: Even today, there is a village name "Saring" bordering the plains of Assam. Of course, we don't know the literal meaning of Saring.

P. Ato. Jamir: Saringrongpang is now called Nagachari and Dokhuka is now called Morani(?) towards Amguri side.

Tako Jamir: This trade and business began after the Aos migrated to different parts of the Ao territory. The trading consisted mainly in exchange of goods and buying of salt.

Tako Jamir: We discovered that salt enhanced the taste of cooked food. Salt was also needed for the *mithun*s that our ancestors reared. It was believed that if an owner of *mithun*s offered salt on the palm of his hand to his *mithun* and let it lick the salt from his palm, the *mithun* would obey all his commands. So, salt became a necessity for them therefore they went out in search of it. That is how trade with Tsümars commenced.

Merazulu Longchar: Let me repeat what we have been saying so far. After we parted ways with the "Sangtemer", all the Aos settled in one place, but gradually they occupied more land and moved to different parts of the present Ao territory. For instance, if the Ungma villagers occupied a certain territory; another lot would occupy the territory bordering their boundary. After they occupied the piece of land, it was divided amongst different clans of their community.

Migration Stories

Guru Sademmeren Longkumer: Though we were told by our ancestors that the Aos emerged out of the earth at Longterok (literally six stones), the contemporary researchers are trying to trace our origin from Thailand.

Merazulu Longchar: Yes. We are trying to trace our origin from Thailand; the research so far has not yielded any definite results. We were told by our ancestors that we came along with the Manipuris as a group but there is no evidence of the time when we parted ways with them.

Visitor: Is there any account of their connection with Tibet? Did the Ao ancestors mention Tibet at all?

Merazulu Longchar: There is no evidence of our links with Tibet but our ancestors did mention Tibet in some of their stories.

Student: Is there any account of a specific place where the Ao ancestors settled down after they came from Tibet?

Guru Sademmeren Longkumer: Aos have no written literature. Whatever they have is preserved entirely in the oral tradition, which depends on the memory of the learned village elders and which is passed on to the succeeding generations. This has been pointed out earlier.

Merazulu Longchar: We have heard that our ancestors had carried Lakep (sea shell) from Thailand and Tibet but there is no evidence to prove that they indeed came from there. Well . . . Lakep in their possession makes us wonder. Maybe they did come from Thailand or Tibet.

Visitor: One of our elders Rongsenwati Longchar from the Yimyu compound told us that the Aos came all the way to Chungliyimti to escape from foreign invaders.

Merazulu Longchar: We do not accept this view. They were not escaping from anybody nor were they fighting with any group. Their sole purpose was to find fertile land and settle down.

Visitor: Were there already people living there when they came or was the land all empty? Did they have to kill the indigenous in order to settle on their land?

Ariyongdang Longchar: There weren't any people living there when they came to settle down. It was a vast jungle. They came a long way searching for fertile land. Let me at this juncture state categorically that amongst the Aos there is no history of any conflict or fight with others. At one point of time, man, god and beasts lived together. While they came along searching for fertile land, we were told that our ancestors were guided by a stick. On their way, they did not meet any people nor did they fight with any group of people. Their sole purpose was to find fertile land.

II

The Emergence from Six Stones

Student: Sir, I have also heard from elders of the Ao belief that we emerged out of six stones at Chungliyimti.

Bendangangshi: Yes some Aos believed that they emerged out of the earth at Longterok, literally six stones.

Longdangsüja Mongru: For a very long time, it was also believed that man still kept emerging out of Longterok but animals used to eat them up.

Guru Sademmeren Longkumer: Yes, the Ao ancestors believed that they emerged out of the earth at Longterok. We do not accept the view of some people who challenge the myth of six stones. We accept the accuracy of the Ao myth which talks of the three male stones namely Longpok, Tongpok and Longjakrep, and the three female stones namely Longkakpokla, Yongmenala and Elongsü. Longjakrep and Elongsü were siblings from Jamir clan, Tongpok and Longkakpokla were siblings from Pongener clan and Longpok and Yongmenala were also siblings from Longkumer clan.

Tongpok married Elongsü, Longpok married Longkakpokla and Longjakrep married Yongmenala. The sons and daughters begotten from these married couples increased the population into thousands and they lived very peacefully in Chungliyimti .

Student: On the one hand you tell us that the Aoer, having come from outside looking for fertile land, got their identity as Aos from the Müraao. Now you are saying that the Aos ancestors burst out from six stones. This is confusing.

Visitor: I too am confused. On the one hand there is talk of migration from Thailand, and, on the other, we have the saying that the Aos burst forth from stones?

Bendangangshi: Some elders have argued that man emerged

out of stone. Had such a thing happened then Ao folk songs and poems would have mentioned about it. Please do not forget that our songs and narratives speak of *Sobatiyaba tsüngrem* (god of destiny) who gives life and destiny to mankind.

Tekatia Imchen: Undoubtedly after creation god made human beings, animals and plants to brighten up the world. This does not nullify our view that man has emerged out of the earth.

Guru Sademmeren Longkumer: The Aos have folksongs to prove that we emerged out of the earth at Longterok. Here goes the song:

Oh ongterokkhu poker,
Nütsüng merijangpenayur,
Terongjunga yuli,
Chungliyimti mesemkoni.

English translation:

Oh! After we burst out from the six stones,
And after the people have come;
Once they gathered there,
We have settled down in Chungliyimti.

In order to commemorate the place, there are six stones erected in Chungliyimti. After emerging from these six stones, we have increased into thousands. We are carefully narrating what we have learnt from our forefathers.

Merazulu Longchar: The Ao ancestors emerged from the earth at Longterok. There were three males and three females. In Chungliyimti, they had built six *Arjus* (dormitories) and one *senden reju* (common dormitory). They made friendship with the other clan namely Mongsener; this is the reason why we call each other *tinu* (best friend) and *tebu* (younger ones). Mongsener also have the same song that talks about how we burst out of the earth at six stones. From Chungliyimti, the Mongsener moved downwards and settled down in "Küpok" for some time.

Later they returned from Küpok to Chungliyimti. Then both Chunglier and Mongsener (Chungli and Mongsen speakers) migrated to Aonglenden, then to Koridang and finally came to settle down in Ungma. This is how migration took place from Chungliyimti to different parts of the Ao territory. Initially, there was only one village. We are now writing Aos history, since we all agree on Chungliyimti we do not look for historical evidence beyond that.

History?

Guru Sademmeren Longkumer: There are so many myths that talk about the origin of the Aos. We are only telling what we have learnt from our forefathers about how the Aos emerged out of the earth at Longterok where they lived peacefully.

Visitor: The reference to stones makes me think. One way of tracing their origin could be the imagery of a rocky terrain such as that of Tibet which they left for more fertile land. The placing of the six stones to mark their origin in the new habitat could be viewed as a kind of link with the ancestral place such as Tibet?

Merazulu Longchar: Some of us thought that surely we could not have burst out of the earth at Longterok in Chungliyimti. So, after consulting with some people like Imtizulu, we formed a committee known as "Mongsen team" in the year 1963 and have been researching since then. We have traced our origin from Thailand. Our research is still on. In spite of this most people seem to think that Ao ancestors had emerged out of the earth at Longterok.

Teacher: I have also heard of stories that talk about how the Ao ancestors burst out from the six stones. However, when they narrate the stories, the elders also mention that they came from somewhere. To me it appears that the six stones seem to have been kept only as a monument to mark a starting point of their life in Chungliyimti.

Tako Jamir: Our forefathers have made a resolution to start afresh their history from Chungliyimti. When they lived in Chungliyimti, they built six *arju* (dormitory) and several *senden reju* (community complexes) in order to discuss and administer their state of affairs. There they have resolutely taken oath to talk about their history from Chungliyimti settlement onwards. Therefore, they have named the three couples as Longpok, Tongpok and Longjakrep. Let me tell you a story. In earlier days, the Changki villagers were more advanced in education. A man from Changki village named Ajangtoi expressed the view that Aos did not emerge from the six stones in Chungliyimti but belonged to the Mongolian race and must have migrated from somewhere. On hearing this, the Aos imposed a fine of Rs. 50 on him!

Student: It is very difficult to say with certainty whether the tribe has migrated. But it is also believed that they came, crossing a river by sitting on the stem of a banana tree. Water is mentioned in the story as well as in a song.

Visitor: One cannot overlook the significance of the presence of the Brahmaputra River in their neighourhood. The mention of water in their songs could suggest that they might not have come from outside. Take the instance of the Khasis who considered their land as sacred. They are so well identified with their geography and their gods are so intimately connected with their environment, it is difficult to imagine them in isolation from their land. In that sense the thesis of their having migrated can be questioned. On the other hand, of the neighbouring Garos, there could be some talk of their having come down from Tibet since not water, but stones play a significant role in their accounts. Similary rocks and stones are very significant in the Ao world-view.

Then there is also the thesis of the geographer who says that once upon a time, Asia used to look very different. There was a massive break, and everything went underwater. The land that we have now emerged from the sea after a massive earthquake.

And think of the view, held by some that the South American tribes of today are actually close relation of ours. However, as scientific research on this is continuing we cannot comment on this. Well since the elders say so, migration in search of fertile land was common among the Aos. This could mean that they did come from somewhere.

Teacher: This being so, some elders today are saying that, the six stones should be looked upon only as monuments.

Tako Jamir: I insist, once a resolution to say that the Ao ancestors emerged out of the six stones has been made and accepted by all, our history has to be based on this alone. If we go beyond that, we can never come to a conclusion. In order to commemorate this event, they have laid down the monuments of the three stones, i.e. Pongener stone, Longkumer stone and Jamir stone (Tongpok Longpok and Longjakrep).

Student: I think having come from outside and settled in Chungliyimti, they knew that they have not come forth from the six stones. So in order to commemorate their history they kept the three stones as a symbolic monument to show that from here the Ao ancestors started their life.

Teacher: They are talking only of the place from where they started. The elders here are telling us that the Ao ancestors came from somewhere but they could not trace their origin from any particular place. Therefore, the ancestors decided not to worry about their actual origin and made Chungliyimti, the first Ao settlement, the starting point of their history and life.

Imtinochet Jamir: We have burst out from the six stones in Chungliyimti. So, we have to tell the truth that we have burst out from six stones in Chungliyimti. This is what we have learnt and talked about for so long.

Teacher: But if we do not go beyond the Chungliyimti settlement, all our folk tales and songs would be rendered meaningless. I have a lot of problems with this.

Visitor: Let us try and clarify the confusion regarding the place of origin. So far we have narrowed down to Thailand and Tibet.

Student: Regarding Tibet, our other informants have told us that they have heard their elders mentioning the name Tibet in their stories. But they have not told us that Aos' ancestors originated from Tibet.

Tako Jamir: Let us forget that. Our ancestors sensed that they had migrated from some other place. That being so they kept the six stones as a monument in Chungliyimti. Just listen to this song:

Oh jena kongko lir,
Tekong tera denka rali;
Lakodongko mener,
Tsüti denka rali,
Tafo melemchetna;
Chungliyimti tekong tsüko,
Sanikvonik dejen atsü yozang talakjokna.

English translation:

After our stay on the hilltop of Jena,
We came crossing ten hills;
Sitting on the stem of banana tree,
Crossed a mighty river,
And could not divide the clans;
It is on the hill top at Chungliyimti,
That the division into clans took place,
Don't forget this law.

This song talks about how our ancestors lived in Jena,* towards Thailand. They came crossing ten hills sitting on the stems of banana trees. This era which is prior to Chungliyimti is known as Longsü otsü or Tarnünger otsü (golden age). The age that began with the Chungliyimti settlement is known as "Lipok otsü".

* Now known as China.

Tako Jamir: Sea shells with which we used to decorate our traditional attire are not available in our place. As the song validates, while they came crossing the mighty river, sitting on the stems of banana trees, they collected those shells from the shore and brought to our place and made our attire with that.

Imtinochet Jamir: During our forefathers time, apart from agricultural work they had no other business like the way we do now. If they had a good harvest, the stock lasted the whole year. If they had a bad harvest, there was a problem of survival.

As has been mentioned, human beings did not actually burst out from stones. But we should now stop talking about from where they came. Our discussion should start with the settlement at Chungliyimti. Their purpose of searching for fertile land was to cultivate the land and have good harvests in the field in order to keep their stomachs full.

Tako Jamir: In our forefathers' time, stone was also regarded as important and it is significant how stone was used by them. However, no songs were sung in order to validate, that stone was regarded as important by them. There are stories about how our ancestors crafted out human images from stones. Also they erected stones to demarcate their boundary.

P. Ato. Jamir: Perhaps our forefathers came and stayed during the Stone Age period. They used stones to trim their hair, to make fire, and used stones to carve out human images from stones.

The Power of Stones

Student: What they are saying is that there is no history of giving importance to stones as such. Stones were used only as tools.

Teacher: But the stones are regarded as their ancestors. They have originated from them?

Visitor: Have the six stones been recognized as sacred? It will be interesting to know if there were other sacred stones besides these six stones.

Student: *Ngayatiya* stone was the first stone god worshipped by the Ao ancestors in Chungliyimti village. There are some important stones worshipped by the Aos in the different ranges of the Ao territory. I can name quite a few such as: Ngayatiyalong, Kivolong, Changchanglong, Longphalong, Ansülong, Longlangpalong, Ungerlong, Küralong and Magibalong.

Tekatia Imchen: Khokalong and Pangchenlong are the Along Tsüngrem (stone gods) that I know.

Longdangsüja Mongru: Longlangba stone god is found in Longkhum village. This stone is said to be the oldest stone god in this village. It is said this stone god used to help the villagers in times of warfare, and brought fame and honour to the people. There is a song sung in praise of Longlangba god.

Oh! longkhum kü yimkongi,
Tsüngrem yimküm mongjen;
Moyatsün sako meya remchen,
Koyimerna tenangshini.

English translation:

Oh Longkhum my village,
God's abode;
The burial place of my enemies,
No villagers should try to invade us.

Arenjenba Ozukum: If anyone disrespected the stone god (Longtsüngrem) he suffered well deserved misfortunes for his act of sacrilege. Lemtutsüpok Long is the name of a stone god located at Lemtutsübo (Lemtur's well) in Mopungchukit village Lemtutsübo was worshipped only by the Lemtur clan. They take the name of the god while holding *antepong* (a cock) "Oh! Ita-anü Tsüngrem (moon-sun god) Yimkong Tsüngrem (god of all), my grandfathers from the Lemtur clan have water gifted by you; they worshipped you in the past we worship you now". He'll pluck six feathers of the *antepong* and an extra feather by

1. Lemtutsüpok Long — The Magesterial Stone God with Moon-Sun overseeing all

saying "if anyone hasn't got, please take. I for myself have got nothing. Yimkong Tsüngrem, Ita-anü Tsüngrem (god of all, moon-sun god) take all these."

Nungshimangyang Longchar: Ansülong is the name of a stone god found in Süngratsü village. This stone god was worshipped by all the villagers for a certain period of time. After a while, the Chungli-speaking people and the Mongsen-speaking people had some misunderstanding over some issues since then the Mongseners stopped going to worship this stone god. But the Chungliers worship this stone god till today.

Arsashi Jamir: Stone worship began when the Aos first settled in Chungliyimti village. Stone god is worshipped in order to invoke blessings for good health, prosperity and plentiful harvests. If this stone god is neglected, he can wreak havoc on the people through his power, cause diseases and there will be no prosperity in the land. At night if he roams around the streets in the village it's a bad sign, very soon someone will die in the village.

Teacher: There is no denying of the sacred status of stones in the Ao world-view after these illustrations. This will become clearer when we discuss the gods of the Aos a little later.

Land and Divinity

Visitor: Respected elders you have all emphasized the importance of land for the early settlers. I wish to know if there are any references that land (*ali*) was considered sacred or precious to them? Was it considered as a gift from God?

Merazulu Longchar: Land was considered neither as sacred or precious, nor as a gift from God, but the Ao ancestors came a long way looking for fertile land. The soil was tested for fertility by digging out a pit and filling it up again with the dug out earth. If the pit was completely filled with the dug out soil, they considered the land fertile, if not, it was believed to be non-fertile. This was based on traditional knowledge, not a ritual performed in order to gauge the fertility of the land.

Guru Sademmeren Longkumer: I disagree. The Ao ancestors believed there is the God Lumong Tsüngrem even in the fields. So, after the work of slashing and burning they always offered *antepong* (cock) and *entsü* (egg) to the field god in order to sanctify the place where they wished to plant their seeds.

Meyawati Walling: I can give you an elaborate account of this; the village priests will survey which field they are to cultivate that year. After they have surveyed and chosen the field, they will observe *Amou* and will stay at home without going anywhere. Once this is done, all the villagers will go to their field to work. After the fields are slashed, they observed another *Amou* with a cock. In olden days, the villagers would go round the village in order to kill the monkeys and also to drive away the evil forces in the village. Further, they observed another *Amou*. The first day they go to the field, they carry an egg. We named it *Alipangpar*, meaning "we began our work in the field which was so far uncultivated". The next two days they will take a cock each day. In olden days, they used to take a dog. During the sowing season, we would take another cock. Once these rituals are done, the entire village will take an egg, a cock and a pig and go to their fields together. We will cook the food in the field. Yes, we too offer the food to the field god. We will hoist six bamboo sticks called *phojong*. Before we eat anything, we will keep for the field god a small amount of rice, and six pieces of meat in one stick and five pieces of meat in another stick. The rice beer will be kept in *amtsang* (container made with banana leaves). They offer to the gods by telling them these two *amtsang* one containing rice beer and the other the fermented rice beer are the end of their offerings. Later, we would cook the pork and chicken and eat the meat. That day, as we were busy with the feast we did not do any work in the field.

We used to share with our neighbours four portions of the meat and the soup we prepared from the pork and chicken. On returning home, we would cut all the meat into small pieces and eat with our relatives and friends. Without observing the *kimem* (being physically clean) we never performed any rituals and sacrifices.

It is believed that god never accepts our offering if we perform the rituals and sacrifices suddenly on any random date. We observed six days *Amou* prior to performing rituals and sacrifices. During this period, we are not supposed to attend funeral services and visit dead persons' homes. We should abstain ourselves from eating and drinking from other people's house. If we have already fixed the date for the rituals and sacrifices, it should not be postponed or cancelled. We observed *Kimou/Amou* either six or seven days or fifteen days or thirty days depending on what kind of things we worship. If any person or household fails to observe the *Kimou/Amou* they die of madness. In order to perform rituals and sacrifices we should first of all speak the truth and keep ourselves physically clean at home. If they fail to perform the proper rituals and sacrifices, god will never accept their offerings and they may have to face the consequences of their actions. Suppose they go to the field without observing the proper *Amou*, they may fall ill or sometimes may even die.

Yabangchila Imchen: When we observe *Amou*, we will put a sprig of *akimeyimlawa* (a herb) in the house compound. The moment the villagers and outsiders see the sprig in front of a house they knew, that family is observing *Amou*. So, without prior permission they will not enter the house.

Visitor: What did the Ao ancestors think of the moon, the sun, the sky and the rain? Did they consider them also as a blessing from God for their survival?

Merazulu Longchar: This I must concede. The Ao ancestors invoked blessings from the moon and sun and land. It was believed that good people are born on earth. Whosoever walked the path of the moon and the sun is fortunate. Whenever they performed any rituals, they hit their spear on the ground mentioning that they are alive because of the blessings from the moon and the sun. The moon and the sun were regarded as the source of their greatest blessings because they knew that plants needed sunlight; and they planted their seedlings according to the position of the moon. Hitting on the ground was a sign to bless the Land. "Tazüng" will invoke blessings in the name of the villagers. It was not done individually.

Guru Sademmeren Longkumer: Yes, human beings alone cannot do anything; they believed that there is a God who is more powerful than they. They knew that without his blessings they are helpless. They planted the seedlings according to the position of the sun and the moon and also by keeping themselves physically clean.

Ritual and Sacrifices

Meyawati Walling: Let me make a point about prayer in this connection. The Christians in their prayer put a lot of emphasis on asking for God's blessing. Hence, we use the term *sarasadem* in the present context for praying to God. We the ancient people invoke God. We don't ask him for an endless demand of blessings but just call out to him. Hence we prefer the term *atakror* to describe prayer and worship of God. In my opinion *atakror* has more weightage than *sarasadem*.

Visitor: So prayer and rituals were an intergral part of the Ao society?

Yabangchila Imchen: Undoubtedly. *Melong* (egg), *an* (hen) and *auk* (pig) were often used in the rituals and sacrifices. In different rituals these things were used differently but sometimes they took two things for the same ritual.

Nungshimangyang Longchar: *Auk* (pig), *antepong* (cock) and *entsü* (eggs) are the three things that were used in rituals and sacrifices.

Merazulu Longchar: We clarified that in order to appease the gods, they used pigs and cocks but the question as to who is going to perform the rituals has not been dealt with. I would like to inform everybody that they would consult the *sangmongtsü* (soothsayer) as to whom to choose to perform the ritual in order to ask God's healing of sickness and also for his blessings. Once a person is chosen he makes himself physically clean, will not eat anything even from his children's house. This is how they maintained purity in order to perform rituals. It is considered more important than animal offering.

Kikasangla Imchen: We used to observe *kimem* for five or six days. When we observed *kimem* and *kitzüng*, we never allowed anyone to visit our home. Our doors were kept shut. The day we observe *kitzüng*, we are not supposed to talk to anyone from outside and allow anyone to visit our house. We would open our doors only the following morning. If there were children at home, they were also locked inside the house on that day. We have to count six days from *kimem* for the day on which we offer the pig to god.

Korakaba Jamir: They are right. There were detailed guidelines for performing rituals. For instance, Anpongsesang (one who is selected to carry the egg or hen basket) was required to observe *genna*. He was not to speak with anyone on his way to performing the ritual.

After the cock was killed he would examine the entrails of the cock in order to know whether their offering was accepted by the god they worshipped. He offered six pieces of meat to god and an extra piece was offered in order to invoke blessings and also to drive the evil force from a sick person.

If crickets and rats are abundant in the fields they perform a different ritual for that too.

Student: Are these rituals and sacrifices performed nowadays?

Meyawati Walling: We used to perform the rituals and sacrifices in the fields. Since we don't cultivate the field, we have nowhere to go to perform the rituals. It has been a few years now after we stopped performing the rituals. In order to perform rituals we should have a proper farm house and a proper field.

The fields where we do not perform any rituals are called *chali*. In this kind of a field, we sow only vegetable seeds and plant vegetable seedlings and not grains. We cultivate only *chali* nowadays. Of course, our ancestors used to perform rituals even at home called *kitzüng külem*. Even this we do not do any more, as we are just the two of us. I and my wife have grown very old. Our contemporaries have all died and we two are left alone. If they were still alive, together we would have done whatever rituals and sacrifices we are supposed to do. Only when there are people, together we can do something. Now, since we are alone and have grown old we are not doing anything.

III

Social Coordination, Ethics and Tradition

Guru Sademmeren Longkumer: Dear student, tell our visitor, culture is holy, if we misinterpret what our forefathers had told us, we are committing sin against God. We have no written script. Whatever we have learnt from our forefathers, we are communicating today as accurately as possible.

Visitor: As students our only interest is to learn about what the Aos and the others thought about the meaning of life generally, how the different communities visualized the ultimate on the basis of which they organized their present life and society.

Merazulu Longchar: Lest we mix myth and culture together, I feel safer to talk about the purity of the Aos' village council and the village administration. For instance I would like to tell you of our ancestors' generosity in not collecting any village tax from illegitimate children, thieves and foolish persons. Of course, in Ao society, they were kept in the lower rung and were not allowed to speak in public.

Bendangangshi: Nowhere were bastards allowed to become members of the village council, they were not allowed to inherit properties, they were not allowed to sleep in *arju* (dormitory); they were not given names and even their friends were unwilling to trim their hair. They lived a very miserable life on earth and as to the land of the dead. Meyutsungba never allowed them to enter the land of the dead.

Visitor: Yes please tell us about the village and the village council.

Merazulu Longchar: Theirs was a democratic form of government; capable persons were elected from amongst the clan members. Eight members were elected by the *kin* (clan) to represent them in the village council.

Student: Are there hierarchies in the village council? Are there rules and regulations to determine who is junior and who is senior?

Merazulu Longchar: There are no rules and regulations that are laid down in the book but there is division of powers in the village administration. Normally we have two councils within a village, i.e Mongsen council and Chungli council. There may be villages which do not necessarily have two councils. In Mongsen administration, Longchar clan is at the top rung of the ladder in the village administration whereas in Chungli administration, Jamir clan is at the top rung of the ladder. Therefore, the Longchar clan takes the head and the bigger side of a pig's thigh which includes its tail as his share and the Aier clan takes smaller part of the thigh as his share. The Longchar clan takes the bigger portion of a pig; this shows the division of powers in village administration. The Longchar clan takes the head of a pig, a pig's thigh which includes its tail and *enkepshe* (a portion of meat in a pig); the smaller clan can have only one *shilep* (a portion of meat) and some meat of *enkepsh*. The eldest man amongst the Longchar clan is elected as *samen*.

Teacher: The Longchar clan takes two *ankepshe* (the biggest share of the meat of a pig) and the other clans share the rest of the meat. Whoever is selected as *samen* (the actual enforcer of all the rules and regulations of the village), the seniormost elder amongst the Longchar clan, is responsible for taking all the decisions in the village council and his word is final.

Merazulu Longchar: His power is equivalent to the power of a chief minister. Similarly, in Chungli administration, Jamir clan takes the biggest share of the pig's meat and whoever is selected as *tazüng*, the actual enforcer of all the rules and regulations of the village is responsible for all village council decisions and his word is final.

Teacher: Let me summarize. The elders have stressed the importance of the village, how the village consists of two kinds of speakers, Mongsen and Chungli. As they have pointed out, the distinction between the two is basically lingual. They both communicate with each other in administrative matters, though each has its own separate council. They also threw some light on the roles of Mongsen *samen* and Chungli *tazüng*.

Tareptsüba: The Longchar clan is the oldest among all the clans. It was believed that Lijaba god accepts only their offering that is why they must be the ones to first approach him. After a sick man recovers with proper rituals and sacrifices, it was considered a blessing. If not it was believed that their god had not accepted their offerings.

Satiba Jamir: All the issues related to the village are to be discussed in the assembly represented by the members from both, i.e Mongsen council and Chungli council but the final decision will be taken by the *samen* from Mongsen council and *tazüng* from Chungli council.

Merazulu Longchar: In cases of conflict within or outside the village, *samen* and *tazüng* will give the final decision. I wish to repeat that matters relating to the village council are discussed in the assembly by the elected members from different clans but the word of *samen* and of *tazüng* is final and both of them take the bigger portion of the meat as their share. However, *Mongsen putir*'s (chief) share is somewhat larger. The only difference between the two councils is the Mongsen chief's larger share of the meat. Apart from this, both the councils enjoy the same powers and functions.

Meyawati Walling: So, amongst human beings there is no one beyond *tsünger*. Nowadays, people don't regard *tsünger* with respect and awe that he traditionally commanded. But, in the tradition he was considered the greatest amongst human beings. In Chungli village council, a person was elected as the *onger* from the Pongener clan and in Mongsen administration the chief was from the Longchar clan.

Visitor: What is the difference between the Chunglier and the Mongsener? Is it only a difference in language or are there more differences?

Merazulu Longchar: Apart from their dialect differences, both Chungli and Mongsen practise the same culture. Inter-marriage between "Chunglier" and "Mongsener" is allowed. Incidentally let me enlighten you all about the closeness of the two. Do you know that people of Langpangkong range of Ao territory cannot speak Mongsen dialect, and yet mostall of the Ao folk songs were composed and sung in Mongsen dialect!

Guru Sademmeren Longkumer: There is a slight difference in the village administrative power between Chungli and Mongsen councils, besides their share of the meat. The Mongsen council chief is a little more powerful than the Chungli council. The Mongsen *putir* (chief) enjoys a share of the meat twice as large as his Chungli counterpart. Correspondingly he has the responsibility to give the final decision and he becomes the chief judge in Mongsen village council. I am sorry if there is disagreement on this, I know I am making a sensitive point.

Suppose both Chungli *tazüng* and Mongsen *samen* retired as members of the village council and become *putir* (a retired member in the village council is known as *putir*), they join the other retired *putir* who are above them. Therefore a Mongsen *putir* who is from Longchar clan can be replaced by another person from Longchar clan if he dies. Gradually, this person will become the second *ong* (chief councillor). As this replacement of person continues, towards the end a *tatar* (headman) will be included. In Mongsen village council, *putir* enjoys his share of meat two or three times than his Chungli counterpart. It is like he eats his share of meat till old age. Therefore, he has the responsibility to give the final decision.

Teacher: I think we should avoid any controversy. Let us turn to Shri Merazulu Longchar for more light on this matter.

Merazulu Longchar: In Mongsen village council, cases related to the village are taken up by the same *samen* and members of the village council. If they cannot resolve the case or are disobeyed by the wrongdoer, the case was taken up to the *putuait* (retired members of the village council) to finalize the matter. If the offender continued to reject the decision of the *putuait*, the entire village would be summoned to give the final verdict. In this way the offender was made to abide by the verdict of the entire village. Similarly in the Chungli village council, cases related to the village were taken up by the *tazüng* and other members of the village council. They followed the same procedure as their Mongsen counterpart. Only legal and criminal cases involving government agencies were taken up by the goan *burah*s at the village level.

Student: What about the much talked about status of the *onger*?

Merazulu Longchar: One member of the council is elected as the *onger*. All the council's deliberations are held in the *onger*'s house. In Ao village administration we elect an *onger* and give the pig's head as his share of meat but he does not enjoy any power in the village administration. The Chungli and Mongsen councils have their own separate *onger*. The fines imposed on the wrongdoer is either a pig or some amount of money which, when finalized, is to be distributed amongst the council members in the *onger*'s house.

Teacher: For the benefit of our visitor here, we must note that every Ao village has its own administrative system. They had their own names for things and their own version of the same narrative. So be prepared for variations from one village to another in term of the village councils. Please continue with the discussion.

Guru Sademmeren Longkumer: In Mongsen village council, only a member of the Longchar clan can become a *samen* or *onger*. In Chungli council, it is only a member of the Pongener/ Ozukum clan who can become an *onger*. He is given the head of a pig as his share. The Jamir clan takes one side of a pig's thigh as his share. A Jamir can become the *tazüng*. The other pig's thigh is the share of the Longkumer clan. If there is no one who is fit to be *tazüng* from the Jamir clan then a person from the Longkumer clan can become *tazüng*. There are twelve members in Chungli village council, two *tazüng*s and ten members. One *tazüng* plays the role of a chief minister and the other that of the home minister. If a person disobeys their decision, the final decision was left solely to his clansmen. And if he disobeys them a second time then the council will take proper action against him.

Student: Not all disputes reach the village council.

Guru Sademmeren Longkumer: Of course. We also have two other ways of settling scores such as *lepchi* and *Alichitepba*. *Lepchi* is considered as a personal matter. It can be between husband and wife and it can be decided by some kind of signs. Village councils are not involved in this matter. All other cases in the village are brought to the village councils and they give the final decision. In case, both the parties are unhappy with the council's decision then they decide to do *Alichitepba* (eat the soil). *Alichitepba* would be the equivalent of a judgement of the Supreme Court today. The village council would give six days' time to the parties after they eat soil. If anything bad happened to either of the parties, that party or person was considered to be the wrongdoer.

Student: I have heard from my grandparents that in the olden days it was the *putir/patir*, who, not only performed most of the rituals in the village, they also took all significant decisions.

Teacher: They were right. In olden days the *putir/patir* performed most of the rituals in the village. Here let me clarify. See, there are different epochs that govern the village administration in rotation. Each epoch has its tenure. Now after the completion of an epoch, a retired member of the village council would become a *putir/patir*. Once a person becomes a *patir* he has no voice in the village administration yet he is consulted as and when it is required. I also know of two kinds of *putir/patir* known as *putipangmi* and *putipungma*.

Arju and Ethical Training

Visitor: Can we now request the elders to enlighten us about *arju*, the popular village dormitories?

Meyawati Walling: The institution of *arju* was meant for the training of young unmarried boys starting from a certain age. The young boys were sent to *arju* and made to stay there for a certain period of time. The boys received training in different skills necessary for the life of the community. The village log drum was kept in *arju* so that if there was any trouble or danger in the village the boys in *arju* would beat the log drum.

Guru Sademmeren Longkumer: The institution of *arju* was there since our Chungliyimti times. *Arju* was established to train the young boys starting from the age of 11 up to 17 years. It was the equivalent of an academy where the youngsters were governed and trained by strict rules. They were taught how to protect the villagers from their enemies. They were put in different groups according to their age. A child of 11-13 years of age was placed in the group known as *süngpur*. The children in this group were assigned the duties of collecting firewood from the jungle to be used at night as torches while fighting with their enemies and also to chase away tigers, to fetch sufficient amount of water in bamboo jars to be used in *arju* and to trim their elder's hair. After they performed their duties as well as *süngpur* for three years, they were promoted to the next rung known as *tenapang*. They were assigned the job of supervisors, to supervise the work allotted to their juniors and also to train their immediate juniors. From *tenapang* they have a few more rungs to climb and were thus promoted to the highest rung known as *sangamein*. They taught their juniors the rules and regulations in *arju*. If there was any conflict in *arju*, it was they who settled the disputes.

Merazulu Longchar: Before a boy became a *süngpur*, he was known as *kongshir* (a child) and *kongshir* was not punished even if he did wrong or made mistakes. Once he becomes a *süngpur*, he becomes a full-fledged member in the village council and he has to take part in all community work without fail. Arju training was not like classroom teaching but the boys were trained and disciplined as they lived together. The day one becomes a *süngpur*, he begins seriously to learn about the history and tradition of the tribe.

Teacher: Allow me to simplify what has been said for our respected visitor. Sir, there are different steps or rungs to the highest in the institution of *arju*. These rungs are named differently in Ao villages. For instance, in Süngratsü village the highest rung is known as *sungchilep tambo*, while in Khar village it is known as *achuzen*.

Temsula Ao: What do we learn in *arju*?

Yabangchila Imchen: In general, *arju* is the place to learn the art of warfare and adherence to village rules. There is no distinction between the rich and the poor. They are also taught hunting skills and also the old songs and stories at the stage of *süngpur*. Being the youngest they were also made to do chores for the elders. Disobedience to the elders was met with punishment. Punishment included, massaging the elders, fetching water for *arju* in the middle of the night and so on. Initiation into the life of *arju* was a difficult process for the pupils. But after they successfully crossed the first stage the boys moved on to the higher stage where they mainly learned about qualities of leadership in the community.

Visitor: *Arju*, then, appears to be a training ground for the young in matters of economy, administration and warfare. They were taught village rules and regulations. Did *arju* familiarize them with the moral codes of the community, the knowledge of the good and the bad, and also the duty of service to others? What about the moral code? Where is the training for moral life? As they said truth is the highest thing. Where do truth and morality fit into the scheme of things, outside or inside *arju*?

Student: There was agreement on the centrality of truth. Truth and God were considered one.

Arenjenba Ozukum: So far we have enumerated the different tasks that the young are required to do as part of discipline and training. Even the most difficult boys whose parents have failed to correct them are taught the correct values in *arju*. All the moral codes are learnt in *arju*. For instance, the values that they imbibed through their *arju* experience are obedience, humility, patience and friendship. There are different words that the young use for friendship. Supposing we belong to the same clan the word used is *tinu* but in Changki village it is *keti*. If the friendship is with a member of another clan we call it *kapu* or *temba*. These terms are used for describing friendship between two people. Variations of dialect as we move from one village to another are common. Friendships, once made, can last for a lifetime.

The Goals of Life

Visitor: I think we can now move on to a more general level in the discussion. One question to begin with may be why is man in the world, at all in the first place? What, in other words, is the goal of human life?

Meyawati Walling: We have learnt that man was meant to be the caretaker of all the lands and jungles on earth and also of the animals. Man (*nisungsangla*) came to earth in order to take care of all the plants and animals.

Merazulu Longchar: It was the ardent wish of every Ao householder to take care of his land. For that reason agricultural activities took central stage in his life. Celebrations connected with harvesting, for instance, so he believed, won honour and esteem during life and after death for himself, and favour of the gods for his clan and village. The giver of the feast may continue performing the ceremonies at convenient intervals depending upon his economic position but this traditionally is done until the harvest is in. These so-called "Feasts of Merit" can be given only by a married man since his wife played an important part in them.

Meyawati Walling: Our elders were also fond of building their homes as lavishly as possible. They reflected their elevated social status in the architectural style and decorations on the house in which they lived.

Walking through an Ao settlement one could tell from the shape of the houses which one belonged to a man who performed feasts of merit. For it was only the rich men who after feasting the village gained the privilege of decorating their house in a particular way. Our grandfathers were ambitious to reach this goal because of the superior position it gave them in the village community.

Satiba Jamir: Let me tell you men were longing for many status symbols besides good housing. For instance, their high social position was also shown by hornbill feathers which they wore on their heads, one for every *mithun* their father had sacrificed or in the case of a married woman, as many feathers as the number of *mithun*s sacrificed by her husband.

Temsula Ao: In an effort to compete for social prestige householders laboured with their families to their utmost to accumulate wealth for this purpose.

Bendangangshi: Getting back to your question about the goal of life I have two likely answers here. Some live to achieve things such as, fame, wealth or satisfaction of passion. Others accept the power called *sobatiyaba*: which means God has created me and I should try to live up to his expectations and lead a good life.

Teacher: Divorcing the pursuit of worldly success from God's expectations from man, may not be necessary. Somehow the two goals are getting distant from each other in the modern times.

Ariyondang Longchar: The highest goal of human life is to attain happiness after death.

Sashimeren Walling: After Lijaba made the world he found the earth very empty. So, in order to protect and guard the world he made human beings live here. Human beings began to worship Lijaba because they believed that human beings were made by him. So man is expected to live in this world having faith in him.

Visitor: Let me try this from another angle. Aos, as we now know, came looking primarily for land, since it gave them life, it became sacred. In the land there are plants, animals, rivers and mountains. So to live in harmony with all these could be the highest aim in life?

Merazulu Longchar: Yes undoubtedly. Their goal was to maintain harmony with nature and also to preserve the land they had occupied. They knew that nature will be of great help for their survival and they were also afraid that mishandling of nature will harm them because of the belief that there is a god residing in everything. So, they regard and respect nature as their friend. This has something to do with the management of the ecosystem as well.

Tareptsüba: Meyutsungba (God) made them for procreation. The highest goal of human beings is to be truthful and to go to Meyutsungba land.

Longdangsüja Mongru: Man is here to glorify God's creation.

Korakaba Jamir: In the beginning, God made two types of *meimchir*, so I think. One is known as human beings, who have a social and a cultural life, and the other is known as animals that do not have a society. To be truthful and to attain salvation was the highest goal of human life.

Satiba Jamir: That *Tiyar* Tsüngrem (God) made the human beings is unquestionable. So is the fact that *Tiyar* Tsüngrem made human beings for procreation. Man is here on earth for procreation, and to nurture and cultivate the natural vegetation God has given to him and to please fellow human beings. Lijaba Tsüngrem will bless the parents if they impart this teaching to their children.

Rongsenwati Longchar: I agree. Man is here for procreation. Ao ancestors came together in a group from far-off places because they did not want to live under foreign rulers. The highest goal of human life is to be self-cultured and to have a society. Society was formed when the Aos were staying in Chungliyimti. An unborn baby starts to have its own culture while he is still in his mother's womb. In olden days, a pregnant woman observed *kimem* (to be physically clean) throughout her pregnancy period, never went out to watch fierce animals killed by the villagers and she was not allowed to go to haunted places because of the fear of miscarriage and the fear of *mojing* (evil) devouring the unborn child. On the third day, after a child was born his father would pierce the child's earlobes and named the child with the sign that the child was his offspring made by his own blood.

Ariyongdang Longchar: When God created the world and he gave human beings the plants and the trees for building houses. Animals have no sense of differentiating his home from others; do not care for their young ones while eating food, etc. Human beings are superior in so many ways. Man is here on earth for procreation. Man is made up of clay. Lijaba made the earth and human beings out of clay. He made the human beings out of clay and blew his breath into it to give them life.

Meyawati Walling: Now, we hear the talk that man is made up of clay but we have never heard of our ancestors talking about what man is made up of. They believed that they were made by God in order to oversee the creatures. In man there is a *tüsaka* (pulse), if the pulse stops then man dies. There is a bird that lived with man in the golden age. She wished to meet man on earth. It is said man and bird met at night and talked each other through *tüsaka*.

Bendangsashi Longchar: Animals and plants cannot communicate with others but humans can. This is one of the reasons why they thought that it is better to be born in human form than as animals and plants.

Sashimeren Walling: Man is better than animals and plants because animals and plants do not possess soul and cannot attain salvation but man can. They cannot communicate and make relations with human beings.

Ariyongdang Longchar: Animals and plants cannot communicate like human beings. Nothing can compare with human beings in any way.*

Man, Body and Mind

Visitor: Our respected elders have brought the focus on man so let us ask the question what is man? Is he a mind–body complex? First what is the word for mind in Ao language?

Merazulu Longchar: Ao vocabulary is very poor. We don't have a separate word for mind. If we wish to say that "your mind is not working", we simply say "your brain is not working". In our language the word *tekolok* (brain) is used for mind.

Guru Sademmeren Longkumer: Brain and heart are like siblings. Our grandfathers used the word brain for the mind. So, whenever we talk about mind, we refer to the brain as we don't have a separate word for the word mind.

Visitor: What about the body? Is there a separate word for body in the Ao language?

* **Sashimeren Walling**: Man is believed to have emerged out of *longterok* (six stones). Human beings worshipped a host of gods like Kini Tsüngrem, Ayim Tsüngrem, Demen Tsüngrem, Atsü Tsüngrem and Tekong Tsüngrem. Hen and cock were offered during worship to Kini Tsüngrem.

All three of them: In Ao language, body means *temang*. Man is equal to body.

Student: I think, if we go by the phonetics, the spelling for *temang* will be *tümang*.

Visitor: Can the same word be used for animal's body? Do the animals have *tekolok* (brain)?

All three of them: We have the same name *tümang* even for the animals. Yes, animals do have *tekolok* (brain).

Teacher: Man's *tekolok* is different from the animal's. But animals do have *tekolok*.

Satiba Jamir: The ancestors were aware of their mental faculties, out of which they believed the soul to be the most important.

Visitor: Is there any difference between the mind and the soul (*tanüla*)?

Guru Sademmeren Longkumer: Yes, these are two different parts.

Ariyondang Longchar: Different people possess different souls. Some possess tiger soul, some have *khangkang* (frog), some *ensülavi* (Jungle cat) and some others *afi* (snake). Those who possess *khangkang* soul will – so we believe – become rich.

Tanüla — Good and Evil

Guru Sademmeren Longkumer: Our ancestors believed that man's body may perish once he dies but not his *tanüla* (soul). Our forefathers sacrificed *mithuns* and cows in order to sanctify themselves from the worldly impurities and also to save their soul.

Tekatia Imchen: The Ao *tetsü-tebou* (ancestors) believed in three different types of *tanüla* (force/spirit) which are present on earth. They are: (i) *tenokiba*, (ii) *tetiyaba*, and (iii) *tesaraba*.

Tenokiba tanüla protects and guides people to the right path. *Tetiyaba tanüla* is responsible for *konangnungsang* (fame and honour) and prosperity as well as for one's sufferings and troubles. *Tesaraba tanüla* is connected with evil deeds, always eager to take away human life. These three forces/spirits are lower than Lijaba (creator of the earth). *Tenokiba* and *tetiyaba* were truthful and *tesaraba* was equivalent to satan/evil.

Teacher: The word *tanüla* signifies not only the individual soul attached to the body, but also spiritual bodies floating around man mostly friendly but sometimes inimical. However let us continue with our discussion regarding the individual soul.

Visitor: Are the terms consciousness, the soul and the self the same reality or different?

Korakaba Jamir: They are the same reality.

Rongsenwati Longchar: A person is born truthful and if he does not turn to evil he remains truthful throughout his life. Our forefathers were always truthful.

Merazulu Longchar: *Tanüla* is very important for the Aos because it was believed that the soul always speaks the truth. Let us take an example. Suppose I fought with a friend and acquitted of the guilt even though I was in the wrong, after death my friend would be proved to be the truthful one because the soul never lies and only speaks the truth. Therefore, in order to save the soul, people never tell lies, beat people, abstain from adultery and keep themselves away from immoral activities. The soul was considered more important than the body. In order to save the soul, they did good work and in return they received blessings. In that sense you may say that the soul becomes more important than the body.

Truth and its Power

Meyawati Walling: Our ancestors believed that truthful ones will go through the hearth of *motsüngba*'s portal and the untruthful ones will go towards the backyard of his portals and will try to enter his portal by clinging on to the wall of his courtyard. So, our ancestors told us to live very truthfully on earth.

Yabangchila Imchen: The truthful ones will meet *motsüngba* in the entrance of his portal, there they will shake hands with him and he will lead them to his hearth to live there forever.

Satiba Jamir: In this context we must remember their belief that there is a *süngtidong* (big tree) standing in his courtyard and every soul has to pierce the tree. Those who succeed were regarded as the truthful ones and those who fail were regarded as the untruthful ones. Men used spear to hit the *süngtidong* (tall tree) and women used *anüm* an instrument used for weaving. Women never killed chicken or stole things because of the fear of missing the mark when they reach *meyutsungba*'s courtyard.

Longdangsüja Mongru: Unseen by the living ones, *tanüla* (soul) of the dead stays at home. Every three years, the soul of the dead visits the living. So, if anyone in the family dies every three years it was believed that the soul of the dead had come and taken him away to live with him. But if the *tanüla* fails to take the living in three or four years he will not come anymore.

Intimation of Death — the Living and the Dead

Student: Can we see the soul of the dead in its bodily form?

Meyawati Walling: Yes, we can see them. If we see and meet them, it's an indication that we will die soon.

Student: Have you encountered any such situation?

Meyawati Walling: No, if we had encountered we would have been dead by now. We know of people who are now dead after having such kind of experience.

Student: Has anybody seen how the consciousness leaves the body immediately after death?

Meyawati Walling: Some people die by telling others "hey, I am going". The living, they said, could see the soul of the dead people only at night. If a person is nearing his death and meets the soul of the dead, it is an indication that he also is going to die soon. Further, while walking in the fields and jungles, if the soul of the dead says the words "hey, I am going" very soon, that person will die.

Rongsenwati Longchar: Consciousness never leaves the house if the living forgets to put away all his belongings. The dead will visit the living asking for his *ami* (spear), *kümbang* (ivory armlet) and *saretpha* (boar tusk necklace). Therefore, they used to take all his belongings to the graveyard so that the soul of the dead won't come and visit them. Of course, his own brothers and sons can inherit his property.

Meyawati Walling: Yes, consciousness leaves the body after death. We were told that some leave happily and others leave reluctantly weeping on their way.

Yabangchila Imchen: Some people die knowingly, telling their dear and loved ones that he is dying. There is an incident that happened lately. The soul of a person told a man who was sleeping in his farmhouse "I am going" and after hearing these words, the man died. A woman named Sademlila saw another woman called Alangtola telling her that she is going by putting a shawl on her shoulders. After three years, Alangtola died. The person Sademlila had seen was not another woman but her own soul! We have witnessed all these happenings which were also told by our ancestors.

Student: Do the souls of the dead know that they are dead and no more on earth?

Meyawati Walling: After the person dies, the soul of the dead will begin his/her journey. On their way, they will come across a river called *Longritsü* and there they will wash their hands. On seeing their hands pale and very transparent, they realize that they are dead and no more on earth. If they die untimely, they resume their journey weeping bitterly. People who die after they finished their life's journey, go happily to *motsüngba*'s portal.

Certain preachers claimed that the world will come to an end after 2,000 years so Everyone should accept Christianity in order to go to heaven. We were told that it was written in the Bible that there would be famine for seven years and prosperity for seven years after that the earth will get submerged under water and finally it with? Everything on it, will burn in a fire! It was an alarming message for everybody and people were shaken by this message. Therefore, whether they wanted to convert to Christianity or not, slowly conversion took place. I guess we have completed 2,000 years. We were told by the converts that the earth will be burnt down to ashes by fire only those who were converted will be saved and will go up to the sky. So, they told us to convert into Christianity in order to be saved. We have been hearing repeatedly about this Christian proclamation since our childhood days.

Student: Did our ancestors talk about the end of the world like Christianity?

Yabangchila Imchen: We have not heard our ancestors proclaiming that the world will come to an end. They were very mindful of the fact that one day, we are going to die therefore we were told to live a truthful life so that we can go happily to *motsüngba*'s portal.

The Scale of Flowers

Meyawati Walling: Our core belief was to live a truthful life on earth so that the day we die, we will go happily to *motsüngba*'s portal. There was a saying how the truthful and untruthful people will face the consequences of their actions in *motsüngba*'s portal. The truthful people will have a decent death. The untruthful ones will die a miserable death.

Yabangchila Imchen: We were also told that *motsüngba* will weigh us on a flower scale. People who weigh less on the scale would die falling from high cliffs and hills on their way as they go about plucking the flowers. With the belief in us that flowers were important in order to add weight on the scale, we used to put flowers on our ears and keep bunches of flowers at home too. Because of this belief we used to grow flowers in our garden and even in the fields. We would wear the flowers in our ears all the time. Without putting flowers in our ears we would never go to the fields. We considered the flowers as an important part in our life. Once we reach puberty, we would pierce our ears to put flowers. Men would put cotton role in their ears.

Meyawati Walling: After we die, we will live with *motsüngba* because he is the God. We have no other belief. If the believers of other religions are also truthful they may go to heaven as they aspire to. If we are truthful we will go happily straight away to *motsüngba*'s portal.

IV

Tiya, the Making of the Individual

Visitor: We have talked about the body, mind and the soul. There is also the very complex concept of *tiya*; shall we talk about it a little?

Guru Sademmeren Longkumer: Besides a mind, a body and a soul, every human being possesses *tiya*. When a person is born on this earth, God gives him *tiya*. So, he has to live his life according to his *tiya*. Whatever *tiya* he has, is his share from God.

Meyawati Walling: Everyone wants to become rich by killing *mithuns* and giving feast to the villagers but not all of us can do so. Only a few people who are destined to become rich and wealthy can do that. That is due to *tiya*.

Merazulu Longchar: When a person is in his/her mother's womb, God makes his/her *tiya*. In olden days, if a person had any special birthmark, he/she was sent off from the village for a while. This was also considered as *tiyatsüba* (a part of his fate). One can make out the *tiya* of a person from his/her behaviour, from his/her style of walking and so on. I can never compete with a rich man or a wise man because I was not given that *tiya*. No matter how much we try to enrich ourselves, it will never happen if it is not given to us. Let me explain *tiya* with a real life example. An elderly fellow named Korachujang saw a mother rocking a baby boy on her back. On seeing the boy, he predicted that one day that boy will become very rich. And so, this man (named Yashitsüngba) is now one of the richest men in Nagaland.

Meyawati Walling: If he works hard, a person can improve his living condition. But no matter how much he tries he will never become rich to share and help the people with his wealth because it is already written in his *tiya* to remain poor. He can share his hard earned wealth in a small way with people but he can never become rich. When he is nearing his death, he will die poor because he was not destined to become rich. No matter how much we sweat and toil on earth, we will never become rich if we are fated to remain poor. Therefore our ancestors told us not to go after things which we are not destined to achieve.

Visitor: Is there such a thing as a strong or a weak *tiya*?

Both of them: It is not a force hence there is no such distinction between a weak or strong *tiya*.

Visitor: Let me recapitulate. *Tiya* resides in human beings whose presence can be read by knowledgeable persons. It's like a distinct identity, a trait or a quality, etc. which resides in you and which some people can make out. We could say that it is inherited. We all have *tiya*, yet the fact that you can discern its presence visible in some and not in others makes it special something like a power (*shakti*). Can we say that though everybody has a body, a mind and a soul, his distinct identity is derived from his *tiya*?

Merazulu Longchar: We may have the same body size and build but everyone possesses his own distinct *tiya* that's how we identify ourselves. Yes, the Aos believe that it is a potency which we find in humans as they live their life on this earth. For instance God has gifted a special *tiya* to *arasentsür* (soothsayer).

Meyawati Walling: If the soothsayer who possesses the power misuses her gift, the power will slip away from her. *Tiya* is given by God to each and every person the day he/she is born. This *tiya* cannot be changed by anyone no matter how much they try. However, if we misuse the *tiya*, then it will slip away from the person. Therefore, our *tiya* and action go hand-in-hand. If we do not share our blessings with others, we will lose our wealth in some other ways. So, we were told to share our wealth with other fellow human beings. Even in our social activities, if we are not given the *tiya* to speak in a large crowd no matter how much we try we won't be able to address the crowd.

Merazulu Longchar: Suppose, before my death, I buy some

expensive parts to be used in a rice mill for my son. If God has not given my son similar *tiya* like mine, the effort will all go waste.

Visitor: Can we regard *tiya* as similar to luck?

Guru Sademmeren Longkumer: *Tiya* is different from luck. The Ao word for luck is *yaren*. We talk about good and bad *tiya* but not strong or weak *tiya*.

Visitor: The reason why I am using the word strong in connection with *tiya* is this. Truth is God. So, truth is all powerful and any and every divine gift must share a bit of that nature. And *tiya* is a divine gift. So can we make the claim that a man with strong *tiya* is nearer to truth?

Merazulu Longchar: If I am truthful, my children will have good *tiya* and if I am untruthful they will have bad *tiya* because it is God who gives *tiya* to everyone.

Guru Sademmeren Longkumer: Yes my *tiya* proves the good or bad deeds of my parents and my grandparents. Suppose, my parents lived a very good life on earth and they were truthful. Then their good deeds will make my *tiya* a good one.

Visitor: What about personal *tiya*? Can I improve my *tiya*?

Yabangchila Imchen: If the *tenokiba* god takes care of us, then we are safe from harm and danger. Whenever the *tenokiba* abandons us we face danger, illness and accident. There is a story. Once upon a time when head hunting was a daily affair, a man went on a foreign trip. On the way, he slept near under a *gelo* tree. At that very moment while he was sleeping, his wife gave birth to a child at home. Suddenly, he heard a voice calling out his name and told him about his child's *tiya* though he was not aware whether his wife had given birth or not. The voice told him this: "Hey *gelolao,* I have given the *tiya* to *nisungsangla*". The man who was sleeping under the tree asked the voice who he was and how he has given the *tiya* to *nisungsangla*. The voice responded that his daughter would be bitten to death by a snake on her wedding day on her way to her husband's village. Later, when he returned home from his trip, he found his wife had already given birth to a baby girl. They decided not to let their daughter marry any man from another village. But it so happened that she was fated to marry a man from another village; her parents were extremely reluctant, but the groom's party convinced them that they will not let her walk but would carry her. Finally, they agreed to give their daughter for marriage. So, as promised, they carried her the whole way. When they were almost reaching the village, she told them that she did not want them to carry her into the village. So, near the village rest camp, they let her down after very carefully cleaning up the place. Out of nowhere a small scrap of a tree skin appeared on the spot where she kept her feet and underneath the tree skin, there was a small snake and she was bitten to death by the snake. Therefore, our forefathers told us that whatever *tiya* we get, the day we are born we cannot escape from it. This story is an example to show that one cannot escape from *tiya* one is born with.

Meyawati Walling: Whatever *tiya* we get at birth from God, we cannot change and we will die of that *tiya* whether it is good or bad.

Yabangchila Imchen: If I am not destined to become rich no matter how much I try I will never become rich. But it is also the case that a man's *tiya* may change.

Merazulu Longchar: Suppose, my parents lived a very truthful life on earth and they were blessed with wealth. After they die, I could not become rich like them. To remedy that, I would observe *genna* for 30 days and will decide to send a *sangmongtsü* (soothsayer) to my parents who are dead asking for their blessings so that I can become rich on earth like them. *Sangmongtsü* would go into her trance, lying on the main pillar post (*tongshi*) in the house for a while. In her trance, she will go and meet my parents. However in spite of the fact that I have sent the soothsayer, if I have committed any sin on earth, or if I have indulged in the worship of *tiyar* known as *tiyar külemba*, my parents would never bless me. One is not to do that for *tiyar* is not a deity.

Kikasangla Imchen: We can only improve our *tiya* if we live a truthful life. Only the truthful ones receive blessings not the untruthful ones. The Aos in the ancient days, lived a very truthful life, Truth was above all for them.

Visitor: All efforts of men do not bear successful results but we should not cry in vain. A life lived truthfully may not bring prosperity without the presence of a strong *tiya*. Having a favourable *tiya* is only in the hands of God, hence man must on his part continue to live truthfully, so say the Ao elders.

Truthfulness, Justice and the Good

Bendangangshi: The tradition speaks of codes of moral conduct in the society. Truthfulness was regarded as the highest ideal, so also obedience to parents and elders. Bearing children out of wedlock was regarded very sinful. So, in olden days people lived a very honest and truthful life. The Aos' ancestors never worshipped any form of idol. Till today in most Ao villages one can find *süngkong* (log drum) which were carved out of a huge single log. The drum was beaten to warn the villagers during an emergency like a sudden attack by enemies, fire breaking out in the village and during solar and lunar eclipse. Log drums were not used as an idol of worship. It is said only the northern and eastern Nagas use the log drum as idol as well as they put *nüpsen* (tattoo) on it.

Tekatia Imchen: People who are truthful are called *yuchasarer* (truthful ones) and who lived an honest life are considered good persons and the untruthful and the dishonest are considered bad. The refrain of their teachings was that one should be truthful in life to get Lijaba's blessings for a good harvest and also for long life for one's children and grand children.

Korakaba Jamir: It was difficult to differentiate between a good man and a bad man on earth. Therefore, the Ao ancestors differentiated between the good and the bad with the help of *lepchi* (a method of judgement practised in olden days). In olden days, a dead body was kept on a bamboo platform. After the dead body has decayed and the bamboo platform fallen to the ground with the remains of the body, if the face of the dead body faces the ground, it was taken as a sign of untruthfulness and if the dead body falls to the ground with the face up it was taken as a sign of truthfulness. In any case the truthful ones are differentiated from the untruthful one by *meyutsungba* in his portal.

Bendangangshi: If there was a dispute about deciding who amongst the litigants was speaking the truth, the ancestors decided such cases by another method called *azüngashi*. The village council will set a date after either fifteen or thirty days depending on the case. During the period if any bad things happened to any party, they were proved to be the untruthful ones. They also used another method called *alichitepba* which involved, eating a bit of soil while cursing themselves. It was a promise to God that if they were wrong they will die. *Idangeter* (village spies) were kept in order to know what had happened after they made their promises. Our ancestors lived an honest and truthful life because of the fear of all these judgements.

Meyawati Walling: During warfare, they engaged in the battles and at other times they worked hard in order to become rich and kill *mithuns*. They believed that all people are born on earth for *yimli* (graciously working for landholdings, village councils, etc.) in order to look after the community and give their best service. Survival depends on the individual's hard work. While in the serving community, we are told not to tell lies and always speak the truth and live a truthful life. Of course, we know that we do not gain anything for ourselves from service to the village; however; it was thought that our purpose on earth is to volunteer for service. We were advised to perform our duty by contributing the *charmelok* (village local tax) and to devote and spare our time for the welfare of the people. It was entrusted as a duty to every individual. To be truthful and to work hard were the major purposes to be fulfilled by every individual on earth. It was advised to everyone to be truthful in all their conduct and not to exaggerate beyond what was being told. We have been following the same advice that our ancestors gave us such a long time ago.

Repjensangba Longchar: The difference between a good man and a bad man was judged by their truthful acts. Truthful ones were appointed to be the leader in the society and they lived a long life. The untruthful ones lived a very short life. Whenever the villagers go for fishing they select the truthful ones to hold the melong (egg) and perform all the rituals and say these words: "O mighty river today I came to this river to catch fish, please bless me". Only after he has said these words he would place the egg and crush the *arü* (a kind of fruit that kills the fish).

Meyawati Walling: Being untruthful is against god's will. Therefore, if we are untruthful, we will face the consequences of our actions. God will shorten our life span on earth and we may meet accidents and die untimely.

Honouring the Warrior

Ariyongdang Longchar: There are two types of men. One who is a coward, who is scared to go to war and the other, who is a brave warrior, is always ready to go to war. Our ancestors told us to be good to the warrior. It is because of his bravery that the villagers were saved from their enemies, from the wicked people and from thieves.

Once upon a time, there lived a warrior and a wealthy man in a village. Their names were Yimchenchang and Menangba, respectively. Both of them gave their services to the villagers in their own ways. Yimchenchang protected the villagers from their enemies while Menangba, who was wealthy, gave food to the villagers. One day, they had a quarrel.

Menangba told Yimchenchang "your victory in wars is all because of my wealth. I provide you with rice and beer which makes you win the wars."

Yimchenchang replied "if I was not there to protect you from the enemies you would have never built houses and cultivated the land".

So the dispute continued. Finally, their case was taken up by the village council to decide who was more powerful. But the village councils could not decide the case because both of them were equally good and powerful. So, they decided to take the help of *ungangla* (a soothsayer) and explained to her what had happened between Yimchenchang and Menangba. When *ungangla* went to Anüngtsüngba (god of the sky) she heard someone singing this song.

Oh Menangba kimako,
Yimchenchang la koa-arong,
Chepshimetang.

English translation:

Oh! In Menangba's courtyard,
Yimchenchang's sword,
Still shines.

On hearing this song, *ungangla* went up to the sky to Anüngtsüngba and explained the matter to him. Anüngtsüngba said

> Menangba is a rich man but only a line of smoke from him reaches us but we can see Yimchenchang's sword everyday in Ao *tongpang* (Ao warfare). Tell Menangba not to compete with Yimchenchang. He could earn all his wealth only because of Yimchenchang.

Therefore, a warrior was considered more powerful by Ao ancestors.

Guru Sademmeren Longkumer: On similar grounds, a warrior was respected more by the people than a *süachir* (person who kills *mithun*). The warrior guards and protects everyone from their enemies, so that they could cultivate the land and earn more wealth so he ought to be respected more.

Visitor: What about the younger generation of Aos? Are they very individualistic or are they like their elders who were truthful, gave service to others, loved their parents and looked after other's welfare and made friendship with outsiders?

Changing Times

Arsashi Jamir: Since Chungliyimti times, the Ao ancestors obeyed and followed the rules and regulations of the village council and were truthful. The more people are civilized, the more they become untruthful. People are led by untruthful rulers all over the world hence today's generation and today's world are very different. Younger generations know only how to eat and drink but not how to work hard and obey their parents. They have become so lazy. This is because of the improper guidance of the parents owing to the fact that one cannot control and correct one's children if one has committed the same mistake. The younger ones always imitate and copy their parents and elders' way of life.

Tako Jamir: I am narrating my personal experience. During our childhood days, we were much disciplined; obeyed our parents and elders, were truthful, hard-working and abided by the rules and regulations of the village council. We acknowledged and respected the village elders. Whenever our parents sent us to another house to deliver a gift or something to the family, and we saw from a distance a village elder, either the village *gaon burha*s or other members of the village council coming our way, we would hide ourselves near the nearest house and let them pass by, then only we went on our way. When we were in lower primary school, we used to sleep in common rooms made separately for boys and girls. If there was a wedding party the school children used to carry water for the party. At the party the volunteers used to come and distribute two or three pieces of meat pierced in a bamboo stick. If we found our teachers, village elders and leaders in the society sitting next to us, we never accepted the food that was offered to us. We used to shy away and would run towards the backyard. The volunteers will follow us. There at the backyard where nobody saw us we used to accept the food and eat it. Today, youngsters are gluttonous. There are so many organizations, for instance, *watsü mongdang* who tries to control and correct the youngsters but they have become unmanageable. Despite all this, whatever rules and regulations, and constitutions we have followed and approved in Chungliyimti, we are still following. For instance, marrying in the same clan is a taboo in our culture. We are still observing this rule. Aos' rules and regulations for the administration have remained the same since Chungliyimti's time. However the younger generations tend not to follow what we teach them.

In olden days, going down to Jorhat was like going abroad. But in today's world going to Kolkata and Mumbai has become like going to Mokokchung town from my village. Distances have disappeared. Within the village, whenever rules are broken, we still take action against the defaulter but in places like Kolkata, Shillong, Guwahati, etc. outside our home state, youngsters demand huge amounts of money from their parents for their education and misuse the money on drinks and parties.

Rongsenwati Longchar: In olden days, service to other members of the community was more important than being selfish.

Meyawati Walling: We should prioritize our service for the people and the villagers. If the village administration is good and strong automatically individuals will also be good. I should not think only of myself but should cooperate and help the people and the villagers.

Yabangchila Imchen: In olden days service to others was the primary goal. Our own work was kept as secondary.

Teacher: He has also mentioned an important point, that is, lack of truthful leaders and leadership amongst the youngsters in the modern times.

V

God, Man and Animals

Teacher: We started with a short historical background of the use of the word "Ao". So far there has been no mention of how the word "Naga" got associated with it. Elders told us of some historians who trace their origin from Thailand, but Tibet seems to be a more popular alternative in their oral tradition. They talked of, how the ancestors burst out from six stones and how those memories are stored in certain areas, i.e. in Chungliyimti. Then we were told about the Ao concepts of man, body, *tekolok* and *tanüla* (soul). An interesting revelation to us was the concept of *tiya*. Why man becomes what he is, is because of the presence of a unique attribute called *tiya* in him which determines the quality of his fate.

Student: You also told us about the good, the bad and the cowardly person with reference to the olden days called the golden age. For now, let us hear from you respected elders about the golden age.

Teacher: There are two epochs. One is known as *longsü otsü* or *tarnünger otsü* (golden age). Second epoch is the period of Ao history after Chungliyimti settlement which is known as "*lipok otsü*".

Sashimeren Walling: In the golden age, man, animals and God lived together.

Rongsenwati Longchar: While human beings were still known as *nisungsangla*, many hill people lived in Makhel village in Mao land. There was no division of tribes and clans.

Sashimeren Walling: Let me sing for you a song describing the period:

Oh menang alivoktemla,
Tsüngrem nozabatsar, akhu tamtabatsar;
Esüng nisungsanglai tezembangangtsaka raoni,

Tsüngrem nozabasangna melong akha ener-er, Ata yongpang amtsarongna zaini;
Akhu tamtabana okmang akha ener-er, Kolakoshika pala aongjangpokna waoni;
Oh! esüng aoyushirla
Sangrü yangka ener,
Jongpongtsüba, sakuyubata nakloroni.

English translation:

Oh! in the beginning when the earth burst out
God was the youngest. The tiger was the middle one
Nisungsangla was the tambu *(eldest). This is how we came*
God the youngest one took an egg basket and went inside the grove of banana trees at the bank of Ata River.
The Tiger carried a pig and went to the deep jungle by coiling his body
Oh! We, the human beings who know how to speak
Compose our songs
Praise each other's trophy heads and make festivities.

Ariyongdang Longchar: Oh! yes our ancestors talked about how man, God and animal lived together after they came together from the eastern side to Chungliyimti. Of the three, God was a bad and greedy fellow and the tiger was gluttonous.

God decided to go on a separate way from both man and animal. He told human beings to worship him with an egg basket and an *auk* (pig) in order to get blessings from him. Then he entered a water pond. Later, he got inside a grove of banana trees. After God left them, tiger also decided to go on its own. On his way, he snatched a pig and took it inside into the deep jungle. From that day onwards the tiger became the owner of the jungle.

Rongsenwati Longchar: There is another myth in this connection. On the grave of an elderly woman a tree grew. Now, below the standing tree a young pregnant lady was seen wrapped up in a misty cloud. She gave birth to a tiger, a man and a god and they all lived together. It is said that when their mother was about to die, they quarrelled among themselves over her properties. So, they went their separate ways.

Visitor: Just a while ago you mentioned the word *nisungsangla* being used for human beings by Aos. Can we discuss how and why the word fell into disuse? But first what does the word *nisungsangla* mean?

Imtinochet Jamir: Both Mongsen and Chungli dialects use the word *nisungsangla* for man. As we have mentioned just now, *nisungsangla* lived with the animals. That era has stories about how *sanga* (monkey) and *nisungsangla* lived as husband and wife. *Sanga* (monkey) was the wife and *nisungsangla* was the husband. They lived together as husband and wife. One day, they had a fight and *sanga* (monkey) divorced her husband. *Nisungsangla* went in search of his wife. On the way, *nisungsangla* saw a cow eating grass. So, he asked the cow whether he (the cow) knows which way his wife had gone. As we have mentioned, during our forefathers time, a statement made was always followed by a song. So, he asked the cow with a song:

Nisungsangla: Masü sünga replao
Küjemsu waya onkhasü?
Masü (cow): Nüjemersü mejemerla
Tekhemeher tzütelangna jebli wakota

English translation:

Oh cow, the one who eats grass
Have you seen my wife?
Whether it is your wife or another
She walked along the river downstream crying.

From our forefather's time, we have learnt that both *nisungsangla* and animals lived together. Even though there is a *tiyar* in man which differentiates them from the animals.

Student: From the stories, we can deduce that initially *nisungsangla* and animals lived together. Gradually the realization came to man that they were different from the rest of the animals.

Merazulu Longchar: We addressed man as *nisungsangla* when he, the animals and God were still together. *Nisungsangla* is a common name for both men and women. I definitely feel that *nisungsangla* is a name given by *temenen* (devil) to human beings. *Sangmongtsü* (soothsayer) heard the devils referring to human beings as *nisungsangla* while having a conversation. That is proof of the fact it was a name given by the devil to human beings.

Rongsenwati Longchar: When man, beast and God were living together they quarrelled among themselves to decide about the division of day and night among them. There was a great debate as to what should be done. *Nisungsangla* wanted to have only day time whereas tiger wanted only night so that he could kill and eat all other animals in the dark of the night. Finally *jenpongno* the bird, said "let day and night always take turns. If there is only light *nisungsangla*'s strength would decline as he will have to work the whole time and if there is darkness all the time he won't have the rest essential for his survival". All the animals and birds approved of this suggestion; hence the decision was taken unanimously. Moved by her sensibility and brilliance, everyone present in the gathering, touched and fondled the bird. This action however diminished the size of the bird and it became very small.

The Private and the Public

Visitor: We have been told that with the advent of Christianity the Aos do not any longer refer to human beings as *nisungsangla* but as *meimchir*.

Student: As Christians, do we not call human beings *meimchir* instead of *nisungsangla*?

Guru Sademmeren Longkumer: During *ong putu* (the golden era) human beings were known as *nisungsangla* and gradually the word has been replaced by the word *meimchir*.

Visitor: I have a twofold enquiry (a) What is the meaning of *meimchir*? And (b) why did the word *nisungsangla* get replaced by the word *meimchir*?

Tako Jamir: In our vocabulary, from one word, we can derive multiple meanings. We think English language is the richest but the Ao language is very rich and we cannot cover the whole range of meanings of a single word. We call human beings *nisungsangla* and also *meimchir*. *Meimchir* also means a couple who make love in private and deliver babies.

Teacher: Human beings as individuals, maintain privacy, and share relationships. The literal meaning of *meimchir* is: *meim* means "under the bedsheet or under the blanket" and *chir* means "what you have or share only with each other". What you have "under the blanket" cannot be in front of the whole city. It's a private domain and leads to the birth of a family. That is how we derived the word *meimchir*.

Student: I too have been told by knowledgeable persons that the meaning of *meimchir* is "husband and wife making babies in privacy". Now, it seems to me that we have two meanings of *meimchir*.

Teacher: This is how I understand it. In Ao language actually the alphabets *ü* decides the meaning of a word. Here we are pronouncing the word as *müimchir* while *meimchir* is a word with different meanings. So, it is context dependent.

Tako Jamir: That is right. We use the same word for different meanings. They differ in their phonology and according to their sound the words carry different meanings.

Visitor: After the advent of Christianity, the meaning of *meimchir* we are told, has changed to "my beloved son".

P. Ato. Jamir: In olden days, our vocabulary was very limited. So we cannot say much about that. During the later stage of human civilization, we started to define words and added more vocabulary to our language and called human beings *meimchir*.

Since the Christian missionaries who came to the Ao areas, and settled in Molungyimsen, a village where people speak the Chungli dialect, they called humans *meimchir* and *meimchir* came to be defined as my beloved son.

Guru Sademmeren Longkumer: God loves all human beings on earth because he is their creator. Therefore, we are known as *meimchir*.

Bendangangshi: Yes. He called us *meimchir* (my beloved child) because we are his children.

Merazulu Longchar: Yes. God loves his beloved children because he made them all that is why human beings are known as *meimchir*.

Tako Jamir: The word *nisungsangla* is new to me. If it was in use in earlier times, they must have got this name from other creatures. Our ancestors called human beings *meimchir*.

Student: Sorry Sir I beg to differ. I have personally heard people from Asetkong, Ongpangkong and Changkikong ranges in Ao territory, refer to human beings as *nisungsangla*. Now, it seems to me that different ranges in Ao areas have different words for human beings. Besides I have a huge collection of Ao folk songs; I remember some songs speak of *nisungsangla*. In both songs and in narratives the Ao elders have mentioned the word *nisungsangla* for man.

Teacher: Why do we prefer the word *meimchir* to *nisungsangla*?

Visitor: Was it because the word *meimchir* implies a special status being given by God to human beings?

Merazulu Longchar: Yes, *meimchir* puts man's status as higher than what it used to be when we used the word *nisungsangla* for man. Actually, when man and God lived together, devil called human beings *nisungsangla*. As human beings began to get civilized, we understood that God loves his beloved children the most. Also because He cannot create anything greater than human beings, we preferred to use *meimchir* for man.

Temsula Ao: *Nisungsangla* and *meimchir*, were interchangeable words from the very early times. But when Christianity came, *nisungsangla* became archaic, it was the vocabulary of the past so people continued using *meimchir*. To give it another interpretation would be a distortion of history.

Visitor: Why did the use of the word *meimchir* continue in ordinary discourse, and not *nisungsangla*? Perhaps the word *meimchir* describes man better, as the Aos understood him, so its use is preferred to the other one. Don't you agree?

Also do not forget now the word *meimchir* means beloved son. This means man has become special. This suits the teachings of the new mores better. Here is the shift from tradition to modernity. The earlier conception of man slowly gets replaced by the concept of *meimchir*. Men get singled out from plants and animals. This is the reason why some of our elders say that men are authorized to kill animals for their food and also other items of creation for his convenience. This follows from his becoming the most important part of creation.

Rongsenwati Longchar: Yes. In olden days, human beings were called *nisungsangla*. With the advent of Christianity, they were called *meimchir*. God made all the animals and plants for him and made him the owner. This doctrine became more powerful.

VI

Human Beings, Animals and Trees

Student: The question that will be interesting now to ask would be what is the relation between men, plants and animals? Men being now called *meimchir*, what about plants *süngdonglidong*, animals *shiruru* and nature *alima yimyayimpu*?

Visitor: Please forgive me for intervening here. Since you talked about friendship between humans something comes to my mind. Can I be a *kapu* (friend) with the trees, plants and animals, rivers and mountains because I care and love them? Is that possible?

Guru Sademmeren Longkumer: In the days when men and animals lived together, a man named Tsüposang could call all kinds of animals by shouting out these words *shitsü pongzü kang, kang* before choosing anyone of them for his meal. One day Tsüposang went to the jungle along with his father-in-law in order to bring the meat home. On the way Tsüposang cautioned his father-in-law against laughing at any of the animals when he saw them. On reaching the spot, they saw a big log lying on the ground. As was their habit, when Tsüposang called, the entire community of animals assembled. A porcupine was the last to arrive; he tried to jump over the log which was lying on the ground but he could not manage to do so because of his big belly. On seeing the porcupine's comical attempt the father-in-law burst out laughing. Hurt at being laughed at, all the animals ran away. To assuage their feelings Tsüposang offered the animals a lump of meat to keep in every burrow. *Tsünü* (wolf) misheard what he said, he heard "a lump of shit" instead of "a lump of meat". Therefore, even to this day, *tsünü* shits in every burrow. From that day onwards there was division and enmity between men and wolves.

Merazulu Longchar: You must have heard of the power of men to transform themselves into animals such as the tiger. There was also a way of getting back into the human form if humans so desired. Sometimes men who transformed themselves into tigers remained so forever; so close was the relationship between men and tigers.

One heard of human beings marrying snakes, birds and tigers; their association was that close. Even today, we have the case of a woman having a tiger's offspring. Let me tell you of an incident that took place in a farmhouse. One night, a woman was sleeping in her field. In the morning, she told her husband off for having made love to her in the open field at night. Her husband was surprised, "No I never come to the field at night. Besides I would never do a thing like that. Don't you know that it is taboo to do such things in the fields?" he said. To trap the visitor they scattered ashes in the field around the farmhouse the following night so that his footprints would be visible. The next morning, they saw the footprints of a tiger! It was thus proved that it was a tiger who transformed itself into a human being and slept with her. In olden days, men and animals lived together, there was inter-marriage with tigers, snakes and birds.

Tako Jamir: In the beginning human beings did not know how to speak, laugh, and even to make loud noise. On hearing the call of the Ohio bird which went "oh ho, oh ho . . .", they learnt how to make loud noise.

Merazulu Longchar: If you are not bored, let me tell you another story of the intimacy between man and animal.

Student: Please sir do continue. I find this most interesting.

Merazulu Longchar: A young Ao girl was engaged to a snake. One day, she went to the jungle with her mother for fishing. After they had spent the day fishing they returned home. While they were half way, her fiance who was a snake came to meet his beloved. So, she sent off her mother alone and stayed back to be with her fiance. Some time passed. While living with him she transformed herself into a snake and she gave birth to baby snakes. As is natural, mother and daughter missed each other. So one day the daughter asked her mother to visit her grandchildren and instructed her to come to the same place where they had gone fishing. When the mother reached the place, she saw her daughter in human form while all her grandchildren were snakes! The little ones embraced and played with their granny's tassel hanging from her shawl. Soon it was evening. When her mother was about to leave for home, the daughter told her mother to take a different route through the jungle because of the fear that her husband would swallow her mother if she met him on the way. Unfortunately, the snake took the same route and reached home after swallowing his mother-in-law. His wife was angry for her husband swallowing her mother and asked him to vomit her out. So, the snake vomited out his mother-in-law and sent her off alive.

Temsula Ao: Animals used to respond to the call of Tsüposang. He could call all the animals out of the jungle to assemble together. This was a power possessed only by Tsüposang.

Guru Sademmeren Longkumer: Yes, they say that Tsüposang had this extraordinary power. Anytime, he called the animals, they assembled at one place but they would not respond to the call of ordinary persons.

Merazulu Longchar: I agree, we should not generalize and say that in the olden days this was the situation but there were some persons who had specific extraordinary powers.

Visitor: Can we conclude from Tsüposang's example that in comparison with others this man had a more powerful *tiya*?

Temsula Ao: I am not sure whether we can tie this up with *tiya*.

Meyawati Walling: *Tiya* cannot be tied up with this extra-ordinary power.

Visitor: Do animals have *tiya*? Can there be any kind of animal who has power like Tzüposang?

Meyawati Walling: It is not the case that all of us possess the same *tiya*. Some people possess what may be called "animal *tiya*". When a person who possesses animal *tiya* or spirit dies, we also find an animal dead either in the field or in the house after a week. That animal is assumed to be the dead person's *tiya*. It is not the case that all the dead people's souls turn into hawks.

Yabangchila Imchen: No, animals don't have *tiya* nor soul and extraordinary power like Tzüposang.

Visitor: Do animals have consciousness?

Temsula Ao: Animals of course have instinct. But I have not heard about animals having *tiya* and consciousness.

Merazulu Longchar: No, they do have a degree of consciousness. Let me narrate a story. One day, a father and his daughter were returning home from their field. On hearing the birds chirping so loudly, father asked his daughter what this signified. She told him that it signifies a big thunderstorm and in order to escape from it they should take the other route. She predicted the thunderstorm from the birds chirping which signified that they were sensing the change in the atmosphere and wanting to share their apprehension.

Teacher: The reason why men thought that they were different from animals was because man has a *tanüla* and animals do not. However, they communicated with the animal, and had inter-marriage with him.

Tako Jamir: There is no story of man having inter-marriage with animals. Of course, there are stories about how a tree transformed itself into a young man, and had an affair with a young lady in a *tzüki* (girl's dormitory).

Teacher: But there is also a claim by some that animals have *tanüla*.

Visitor: May be that is with reference to the "golden period" when man, birds, animals, trees and mountains all lived together in harmony.

Tako Jamir: What we have said in the beginning is true. When man observed that their nature was different from that of the animals, they broke away. They had a meeting on an *arsalang* (cane platform) and decided there that they are the *tambu* (elders) and their decision was validated with a song. I will sing for you this song later. For now allow me to clarify this point.

Our forefathers wondered as to who were the eldest of the three, the evils (*menenmojing*), the wild animals (*aremshiruru*) or the human beings (*meimchir*)? They also believed that human beings were one among many creatures in the world. When they raised the question of who is the eldest among the creatures in the world, they wondered whether wild animals socialized, had a culture and what their manner of eating and drinking was. Second, they studied the behaviour of all the evils (*menenmojing*) before concluding who is the eldest among the creatures in the world. Though human beings are not very different from the animals, they thought that human beings had consciousness which is lacking in animals. They also observed that animals sleep only in holes and ate raw food. On observing the differences between animals and men our fore-fathers gathered together and had a meeting on the *arsalang*.

Teacher: This *arsalang* is a platform where they assembled together and debated on important issues pertaining to their life and discussed about ways to move forward. Initially, they thought that man is also a kind of animal. As time went by, they began to suspect that they were different from the animals. Therefore, they assembled on the *arsalang*, to decide, discuss and debate who the *tambu* is.

Tako Jamir: On that day they decided that human beings were the eldest and they sang a song which I will sing for you now:

Longterok khu poker
Shiba tambuher, shiba tanubuer memetetkhani

Keyi temtaba khola koshi memetet aongdemang nemrebtsuokoni
Tsüngrem talak nungba melongsang enerer amchirongkha umshia okona.
Pa külemtsübo süngpok longtentsudang bena arungna.
Aji akiang meimchiri nisha tambu ata lidi.

English translation:

After we burst out from the six stones
We did not know who the eldest and the youngest was
The Tiger who does not know how to coil his body flattens the whole jungle
God the youngest one has taken a fire torch and gone inside the bushes of banana trees
In order to worship him, do take süngpok longtentsudang *(a variety of ginger) which has a strong fragrance.*
This is the reason why man thought that he is the tambu (eldest among all of them).

After this song was sung they realized that though human beings are no different from the animals, yet they are gifted with an understanding lacking in animals and from that day onwards they decided that human beings are the eldest (*tambu*).

Tako Jamir: The statements of our forefathers were always followed by and validated with a song.

Teacher: They thought that human beings were the eldest of all the created beings like plants and animals. However, in order to come to this conclusion they employed a process. They held a meeting on an *arsalang* (cane platform) and discussed their observations about animal's behaviour like the way they ate raw food, never bothered to go back to their own homes and lived only in deep jungle, etc. Therefore, they concluded without pride that level of understanding of human beings was higher than that of animals.

Student: Human beings consider themselves as one among the created creatures on earth. They made a comparison between

2. Solar Eclipse

the animals, plants and human beings, and having observed that human beings possessed consciousness which was lacking in animals and plants, came to the conclusion that human beings were the *tambu* (elders).

Teacher: What follows from all that the elders have said so far is that although the ancestors knew the difference between men, animals and plants they did not think that man was suprerior to the others.

Visitor: The translation says that in the beginning, there were plants, animals and human beings.

Teacher: Yes and in order to prove themselves as the *tambu* (elders) men employed a process to really confirm that they were the elders. I think that is very important because at first they look at themselves, and when they look at themselves they have the awareness that they were with others; the song specifically says, "we are one of the animals". The poet (man) is not using the word "same". We are one of the animals is the exact translation of the song.

Teacher: You should also be careful about the concept of *tambu* (elder). It is not to be understood in a rigid way. For instance, I am elder by birth to you and you are therefore younger. *Tambu* can be anyone who has greater understanding at a given time. So, the concept of *Tambu* does not imply that man alone is *tambu*.

Student: For instance, in a particular situation, man can be *tambu* but at other times, it could be a tree that is *tambu*.

Animal to Man

Visitor: Forgive me for voicing my opinion at this juncture. Can I interpret this step by men as an act of self-centredness, an assertion of their ego?

Student: I understand the transition in this way, when we talk about the concept of man we talk about *tambu*, but *tambu* should be understood in terms of more responsibilities rather than superiority. However, it is during the transition period that man perceived himself as superior. *Tambu* understood as the elder is when man was conceived as *nisunsangla*.

Student: I am glad the elders have talked about some kind of consiousness common between man and animal. For we have accounts about the tiger soul from so many villages. How is this possible if they have no soul at all?

Temsula Ao: You are mistaken. Let me explain. You see in our tradition the soul is attributed only to man; man has more than one soul. Tiger soul is one of man's souls in the form of a tiger, it is not the other way round. It is not the soul of the tiger but it is the form of the tiger which man's soul can assume.

Visitor: I have a question here. See an exception: man at times can transform his own soul into the form of a tiger. When he becomes the tigerman what happens to the tiger?

Temsula Ao: Yes, the man's soul assumes the form of the tiger for that duration but there is no corresponding soul in the tiger. It's like many of the beliefs all around the world that a man can possess more than one soul, whether in the form of tiger or a frog and so on. In this tradition the tiger is singled out among other animals.

Sashimeren Walling: Let us continue with the discussion. It was believed that big animals like python and elephant can understand human languages. Whenever men met such creatures, they requested the animals to give way.

Bendangsashi Longchar: Though there are no records of words spoken by animals and plants to human beings but as they continued to live together on earth, they considered the animals and birds behaviour as significant, and acted on it.

If God made all the animals and plants speak the same language human beings won't be able to tolerate them. Therefore, he made them communicate with human beings through a sign language. If a *pentsü* bird comes to our *chupang* (a raised platform) and say *touhi, touhi*, etc., it indicates sickness in the family. If the bird just chirps, it is taken as a sign of blessings. They offered pigs and hens in order to get rid of their sickness. An elephant told the other animals that if they gather together and bite him he will care the least about their actions. When they bit him he shook his body showing not an iota of pain. Finally he landed in an argument with an *asüngvong* (name of an ant) who challenged the elephant and told him "you won't be able to defeat me". The elephant accepted the challenge. The *asüngvong* got inside the elephant's nostril and crawled around in it. Elephant surrendered to him with these words "I will accept you as the eldest one, please do come out of my nostril".

Ariyongdang Longchar: Ao ancestors believed that during lunar and solar eclipse the tiger bites the moon and blackens it. Therefore, during lunar eclipse *arju* people used to beat the log drum loud in order to scare the tiger away. It was also believed that if the villager could successfully scare the tiger away, there will be prosperity in their land. And if they would not beat the log drum the blood from the moon will drop in their land and there will be disease in the land.

Tekatia Imchen: Suppose *jongmeja* and *pehya* birds fly and chirp on their right while they walk in fields and forests, it was considered as a sign of blessing and if they chirp on their left side it was considered as a sign of misfortune. Here is the true story of the widow of Penduchepchep who went to her field on the eighth day after her husband's death. That day she saw two birds, *yimpha pentzü*, a bird with no tail, and *diphu pentzü* which had a long tail. The *yimpha* bird communicated with her, sharing her sorrow and she described the incident through this song:

Jemer tsüyujoker-er
Ni tanepang temlu laina;
Yimpha pentzü anüzüko tsünglanaka,
Molulaka kapza,
Ni kijanala demen mezümkada sarorta.

English translation:

After my husband's death,
This morning I went to the field;
Both the yimpha pentzü *and* diphu pentzü *(birds) chirped at me,*
You lonely one,
You alone, how will you now cover the entire field.

Repjensangba Longchar: One day human beings saw the hornbills gathered together in a place. They bathed and hovered around the trees for a few days. On the sixth day, they took a bath and flew away. Henceforth, human beings started to imitate them and observed a mourning period of six days when a person dies. This is one example of what human beings have learnt from the birds.

Satiba Jamir: Let me tell you about snakes. As you all know there are different kinds of pythons. If a bad python blocks our way, it was considered a sign of bad luck such as indicating a death in the family. If they met a colourful python on their way, it was considered a blessing. Yes, a python seldom comes or enters the house where human beings live. If that happens, it indicates danger at home. It was also believed that if a person kills a good python, he was blessed with good fortune in his lifetime. And, if a person met a bad python while walking in fields and forests, it was never killed because of the fear of misfortune in the family.

Bendangsashi Longchar: There are two kinds of *alisa* (python) one kind of *alisa* is taken as a good sign and the other as a sign of misfortune and bad luck. As has been pointed out suppose a person unknowingly killed a bad python in the jungle, on returning home he will die immediately. A python with vertical red stripe on its neck is considered bad and fierce. But if it has black stripe, it is considered a blessing. *Alisa* lives only in deep jungles, in big rivers and in haunted places. If we watch this creature for a long time he will bewitch and swallow us up. We were told not to watch this creature for long.

Human beings can communicate with *alisa* and block his way. They utter these words before *alisa avo tsüngrem nang ayak yengatsümerer ayak sayang* (You are my grandfather's god; I want to have a look at your colour stripes. Please show me). As mentioned above, there are three different kinds of colours: bloody red, black and yellow. Without moving his body he will show all the three colours one after another. If the person wants to kill *alisa,* he'll place a log near him and will tell the *alisa* to keep his head on the log after which he will kill him. After it is killed, he will cut the body into six pieces and throw them away at different places and return home. When *mojing* comes at night to enquire about the killer, on seeing the body parts scattered here and there, he fails to identify the killer. When a person cannot kill *alisa* by himself he says these words, *avo tsüngrem ni akina ami tsaotsükar raroer* (my grandfather's god, stay here. I'll go home and bring some more people).

It is said that the creature waits in the same place for many days till the person releases or kills him. So from the olden days till today people never make the mistake of uttering such words before *alisa.* If he stops the *alisa* he has to return the same night along with other people. If he has no intention of killing the creature he says these words, *avo tsüngrem nang etang nümongchena wachokang* (my grandfather's god, go to your place from where you have come). It was believed that killing *alisa* which carries *awa* (magic) brings prosperity in the life of the killer. They would dip the *awa* in fresh milk and leave it for the night. Next morning, if the milk became reddish in colour, it was considered a bad sign and if the milk remained white it was considered a blessing.

Korakaba Jamir: Human beings were scared of the tiger and the elephant.

Satiba Jamir: Not of the elephent only the tiger. They were scared of the tiger because it kills both human beings and domestic animals in the village. Young boys used to go hunting tigers in the forest. Man and snake were enemies. Men try to kill all kinds of snakes wherever they meet them and the snakes too bite the heels of human beings as and when they can.

Merazulu Longchar: In Khezakhenoma, a man from Longchar clan saw a frog sitting on a stone holding a grain of rice in its mouth. They took the grain of rice from the frog and sowed the grain in the field. They discovered that whenever they left the freshly harvested rice to dry in the sun on that stone, the quantity of the rice doubled. A frog's coming to their courtyard was considered a blessing.

Bendangsashi Longchar: Here is a story (as told to me by the grandson of the man from Longchar clan), about a rat who came to the house of his grandfather and told him that he would bring for him grains of rice from far-off places provided he gave the rat in his house a decent burial by wrapping his body in a shawl, after his death. Grandfather acceded to his request. In order to test his grandfather, the rat pretended to be dead near the main entrance of his house. His grandfather thinking he is dead threw the corpse in a drain with his stick. Immediately the rat got up and cursed all human beings with these words, "From now on you are going to eat only my leftovers from *tsang fung* (rice basket), *alu* (field) and *aning* (basket kept for storing grains in a granary)". And this is so till today.

Sometimes animals transformed themselves into human forms and mingled with them.

Repjensangba Longchar: Human beings were scared of tigers because the tiger used to kill both human beings and other animals. But foxes were a different class. *Shirung* (fox) was regarded as a cunning animal. There are so many fox stories. A cunning fox used to go to the king's garden and used to eat up all his *nabakvo* (a variety of bean). One day, the king decided to kill the fox so he went into his garden to catch the fox. Every time the king touched the fox, the fox would say "Oh king you are touching the *nabakvo* and not me". Then the fox said to the king "If you want to trap me hang two baskets of dry fish on either side, put the chaff on the ground and let me jump from the top. While I struggle to remove the chaff from my eyes you can trap me." Since the fox was so cunning, he suggested to the king his favourite food, i.e. dry fish in order to deceive the king. Hence, since time immemorial, our forefathers speak of *shirung* as the most cunning of all animals in the world. If human beings had cunning similar to that of the fox they were called fox too.

Tako Jamir: Our forefathers thought that animals did not have *tanüla* which men had. When animals die, that is the end of everything for them.

Visitor: So, the animals do not have any connection after life, as in the "land of the dead"?

All three of them: The concept of life after death in animals is not there at all.

Visitor: But some of the legends, myths and knowledgeable persons talked about a dog accompanying the elder to the land of the dead.

Fruits of Action

Guru Sademmeren Longkumer: Whatever actions we do on earth we reap their fruit in our next life, was the belief system of the Aos. For example, a person who killed *mithuns* while living on earth, after his death the souls of these animals followed him and tried to hit him on his way to Meyutsungba's portal. So, whenever they killed a *mithun* a dog was offered along with it so that the dog would guard and protect him on his way to Meyutsungba.

Student: This concept is different. Suppose, a man dies and his *tanüla* goes down to the land of the dead, if he had stolen a pig, a dog or anything for that matter while he was still alive, then, on his way to the land of the dead, those animals would follow him and be visible to others so that he could not hide his sin. This does not imply that animals have *tanüla* and their *tanüla* follows them. There is no doubt that animals have life but there is no conception of *tanüla* in animal.

Visitor: What about plants and trees? Do they have *tanüla*?

Yabangchila Imchen: Not at all.

Visitor: What about consciousness? I ask this question because there was communication between man, animals and plants in the golden age. Could this be possible without consciousness?

Tako Jamir: In *longsü otsü* (golden age) men were not aware of themselves. They simply lived.

VII

The Many Souls of Man

Visitor: The *tanüla* (soul), it is said, never dies and goes to *asüyim* (the land of the dead). The immortal soul leaves the body and goes to different destinations as per its deeds when it was attached to the body. What to me is not clear is this: There is a judgement for the good and bad deeds in Meyutsungba's portal. Each soul is to carry the mark of its deeds, good or bad. How does Meyutsungba recognize the different souls? Do they retain their individual identity even after death? We have the word *karma*, a word for the effects of deeds that the souls carry as they approach the God of Death in the larger Indian tradition. What form does the soul take as it travels down the road with the weight of its *karma*?

Temsula Ao: Here let me tell you something which might throw some light on the status of the soul after death. The Aos believe that every individual has a number of souls, men six and women five. Of these the principal soul is the one which sustains the life-force in the person. When this soul departs from the body, then the person dies. The next important soul, it is said, turns into a hawk and flies away. When death occurs a hawk usually comes and sits on the person's house or simply hovers around in the neighbourhood. It is believed this soul also goes to the land of the dead and visits the earth in its hawk form from time to time.

Student: Thank you for the additional information but the question still remains. How does one identify a particular *tanüla*?

Guru Sademmeren Longkumer: God can identify the different souls, human beings cannot. But humans in their dreams can find the dead person in his former shape, wearing the same kind of dress he wore when he was alive and with the living.

Merazulu Longchar: When I die, my parents and relatives who had passed away earlier will come to take me. My soul takes my earthly identity. Suppose, I was a warrior on earth, then I will go as a warrior to the land of the dead, if I am a poor man on earth I will remain the same even in the land of the dead. In Meyutsungba's portal, whatever things one has stolen in his life time will be revealed and will be given back to him with these words, "here are all the things stolen by you". Out of fear for this humiliation, and also to save the soul from all other sins people try to do good things and live a truthful life on earth. Please remember, in the land of the dead, there are places for both good and bad people. The Ao word for the bad place is called *sangsünü*. Truthful ones will enter Meyutsungba's hearth and the untruthful ones will roam in the thick prickly bushes in *sangsünü*.

The Country of the Dead

Visitor: Do all beings go to the land of the dead? I thought that only good people go to Meyutsungba!

Imtinochet Jamir: Both the good and the bad ones go to the land of the dead. We do not know whether the good and the bad people live together or not. However, the good and truthful people go straight to Meyutsungba's portal with all their glory and honour whereas the untruthful and bad people go to the back of Meyutsungba's home.

Merazulu Longchar: All the souls of the dead go to *asüyim* (land of the dead). Suppose, a person had committed suicide, even in the land of the dead his soul will always wear the rope on his neck and his hawk will do the same as the hawk hovers around the place.

Rongsenwati Longchar: There are different causes of death. Some people will die by the sword, some will die of drowning in the river and some will die of falling from the hilltop. Whatever the case may be all the souls of the dead go to Meyutsungba's portal. The dead bodies of people who were killed in landslides or by tigers were not taken back home but burried in the place where they met their death. They make graveyard for them by hoisting the *rongmi* (ornamented spear made of bamboo). They observed a mourning period of six days for men and five days for women as the bodies decomposed.

Imtinochet Jamir: A year after my father died, we consulted a soothsayer (*arasentsür*) in order to find out what caused his death. In olden days, if the soothsayer was not in my range or village, we used to go to other ranges of Ao areas in search of a soothsayer. We believed that the soothsayer was a mediator between the dead and the living. She will go into a trance and ask the dead person what was the cause of his/her death. In my dad's case, she told us that he was killed by *yimdong tsüngrem* (bad force in the street). Also tortured by *temenen* in his field, he could not save himself from the *temenen* and therefore died.

Bendangangshi: With the death and the decay of the corporeal body the soul starts its journey towards the land of the dead. There are so many views about the exact location of the land of the dead.

Tareptsüba: I too have heard of this. On his journey towards *asüyim* (land of the dead), the soul reaches a stream called *longritsü*. After having a bath in the stream as he/she continues his/her journey, he/she will come across another stream called *sangphitsü*. In that stream, if his/her hands look pale and thin and don't hold the water that drips through his/her hands he/she comes to know that he/she is dead and decides to obey Meyutsungba's command.

Bendangangshi: When the soul of the dead person enters *diphu lima* the living relatives begin *Tsüngzü* (offering) by telling the soul of the dead person, "Climbing up the mount Diphu you must be very tired, so your mother, father, sisters and others are massaging your legs". After the massaging is over, they wrap the corpse with a piece of cloth and tie small pieces of flesh or cooked meat to the cloth saying once again, "This meat is from your father, mother, aunt and sisters and do share this food with your grandparents and relatives after you reach Diphu land". Once *tsüngzü* (offering) is over, the family will release the soul from the house. If the soul of the dead person stays in house it was believed that there would be another death in the family. Only on that day, in Ao culture women are allowed to use shields as they release the soul from home. Finally, they pierce a *khüling* (seeds of the sword-bean creeper) by *nü* (spear) and send it along with him/her to give to *lendangsangji* (street bastards). It is said Meyutsungba (god of justice) never allows street bastards into the land of the dead. *Khüling* was taken for street bastards because the things sent along with the soul of the dead person get robbed on the way by the street bastards.

Temsula Ao: Here I beg to differ. Good and bad places such as heaven and hell we have started talking about, only after conversion to Christianity, earlier we only talked about *asüyim* or the land of the dead.

Yabangchila Imchen: In my Longkhum village, there is a place which we believe to be the bath pool of the dead people. It is 2 to 3 km away from the village. This is a plain area; at some places if we stamp our feet, it makes a sound that is believed to be that of *longritsü* (bitter water). People who live close by have heard the sound from the *longritsü*. We called that plain *asürkülang tokchen*. When people hear the sound from *longritsü* they think somebody must have died.

Meyawati Walling: In that place, there is a flat stone, and on top of that stone there is also a smaller one. The villagers do the jhuming near the *longritsü*.

Yabangchila Imchen: After death, the souls of the dead live together in *asüyim* (the land of the dead) where there are festivities throughout. A story: A dead man's soul had asked his wife to send him his *arong* that he kept at the bottom of his cane basket. And the *arong* did come to him. There are songs that validate the story.

Meyawati Walling: Let me tell the story. Once the wife of a dead man sent a *ratsünlar* (soothsayer) to the land of the dead in order to know what her husband was doing in *asüyim*. The soothsayer returned and conveyed the message from her husband. He told her that there are festivities and dancing in the land of the dead so he needs his *arong* in order to go dancing at the rich man's house. Therefore, he told his wife to send him the *arong* (name of attire used for dancing made of dyed goat hair) which he had kept at the bottom of his cane basket. Sure enough the wife found it in the cane basket and so she sent it to him through the soothsayer.

Longdangsüja Mongru: Yes. They want their belongings even after death. There is a song that goes like this:

Akhumliyimla Sako terayuka Jongpong terayimsü
Bendanger amongra medem
Takula Diphulimako anapensosaka lano

English translation:

In this world, even if we possess honour and glory
Staying here on this earth feels like being a stranger who is just a passerby.
In the land of the dead, I am living as if I have been born twice.

Yabangchila Imchen: Further, we were also told that if the soul of the dead stumbles on a stone or a log they will turn either to stone or log whichever they happen to stumble on. Our ancestors told us not to ill-treat the animals because in the land of the dead we will face the consequences of our actions. If we ill-treat them, we are made to eat their shit and the animals will take revenge on us by beating us in the same way we did to them.

P. Ato. Jamir: The untruthful one will also carry all the burden of his dishonesty to the land of the dead.

Visitor: After they go to the land of the dead, will they meet their loved ones who have gone before them?

Imtinochet Jamir: They meet all the dead people in *asüyim* (land of the dead).

P. Ato. Jamir: In the funeral ritual, we mention the names of the dead family members, relatives and loved ones who are already dead and tell him to go down happily in search of them.

Yabangchila Imchen: Before we bury the dead body, we keep all the dead person's belongings one after another near his coffin in a *molok* (a basket made of bamboo) and tell the soul of the dead not to forget his things. However, we do not put any ornaments in the coffin. We even take off the ornaments the dead were wearing at the time of their death – just before they die. Of course, we put away some things for the dead; things such as we need for daily use like a comb, threads of different colours, etc. We place these things near the head of the dead. The valuable things that belonged to the dead person are equally distributed amongst his/her kin.

Meyawati Walling: *Tsünglir* is a procedure we follow with the dead person during the funeral rites. We put for the dead person a chicken, a small amount of meat, fish, rice and rice beer all properly packed and put away in the *molok*. We tell the soul of the dead person that his parents, family members and children, etc. who were dead before him will be coming to meet him half way so he must share all these things with them.

Yabangchila Imchen: We pack food separately for him by telling him "this package is only for you". We call this procedure *tsünglir*. In day-to-day life, if we pack small amount of food, we name it *tsünglijem*. If a man had killed *mithun* during his lifetime, we kill a dog on his behalf at his funeral, near his coffin and say: "On your way, if the *mithun* tries to hit you, let this dog bark at the *mithun* and drive him away in order to protect you". However, we never put the dog inside his coffin. The villagers would kill even a cow for the soul of the dead person if the person had given feasts to the villagers while he was alive. Suppose, the dead person did not give any feast and had not killed any *mithuns* in his lifetime then we would put away only chicken.

Between the Living and the Dead

Meyawati Walling: *Ratsünlar* (soothsayer in Mongsen dialect) was the mediator between the dead and the living. Once I had fallen ill. The *ratsünlar* found out the cause of my illness by shredding banana leaves, a practice prevalent among soothsayers, and told me that I was caught by *mojing* (evil) in the field and that caused my illness. In a second incident I got rashes in my body which was very painful. When I touched the rashes with my fingers, the pain was unbearable. I was told by the soothsayer, while I was walking in fields and forests, *mojing* put some dirt in my body that caused the rashes. She massaged my body with *changchangwa* (name of an herb) and sucked out the rashes with her mouth. Thus I was cured from the rashes.

Visitor: Do the dead possess the same body which they had while they were alive in the land of the dead?

Imtinochet Jamir: Yes, the soothsayer informs that the dead person had the same appearance as when he was alive on earth.

Tako Jamir: Our ancestors believed that in the land of the dead, there is a village, where all the souls of the dead live together. Suppose, I got married to three women while I was on earth, but in the land of the dead I would stay with my first wife. Moreover, my wife would take the help of a soothsayer to find out how her husband is doing in the land of the dead. The soothsayer would go into a trance and communicate with the dead person. There is a story about a man who sent a message through a soothsayer. He had forgotten to take his *arong*, an ornament worn by men while dancing. So, he asked his wife to send him the *arong* which was lying in the cane basket at home. He told her that he needs *arong* to go dancing at the rich man's house in the land of the dead. His wife wondered about the rich man's house where there was feast and dancing in the land of the dead. However she kept the *arong* in his graveyard and she sang a song.

Asüyimkala Shir jongpongdir lirakha
Changyatsudong pangna arong mejenjangdangta
Sangpongba dang shilema

English translation:

In the land of the dead, in which house there are feasts and dances.
My husband sent me a message to send his attire
He sent this message through the soothsayer.

Her husband's message through the soothsayer made her believe that there are indeed feasts and dances even in the land of the dead. This was the evidence to our forefathers to believe that the souls of the dead live the same kind of life even in the land of the dead, in the same physical form like we do on earth.

Bendangangshi: Here is a story about a couple named Yimoti and Yimrenla that speaks of life after death. While he was still alive he told his wife not to re-marry anyone after his death because he will return soon to unite with her again. She promised her husband that she would never remarry. She waited for a very long time, but he never came back. One day, she went to her mother-in-law's house and told her about the promises they made to each other before her husband's death. She also expressed her plan to re-marry because she could not wait for her husband any longer. Her mother-in-law was very optimistic, she persuaded her daughter-in-law to wait for her son for some more time. Finally, they decided to send *arasentsür* (a female soothsayer) to *asüyim* (land of the dead) to know what all was happening in that part of the land and to get the information on her husband. When the *arasentsür* met Yimoti in the land of the dead, he sent this message through a song, and also asked his wife to send his *arong*, which she had forgotten to put for him, because his attire was incomplete to go for dancing in the land of the dead. After she listened to his song she too sang this song.

3. The living and the land of the dead

Yimoti – Akümli yimla tenkalim lima,

Sako tera yokna;
Jongpong sünga yokna,
Bendanger amongra medem,
Kü dangila oro lima ayidemenko;
Par ajurur
Kuaarong mapang khano;
Sarür ejem süngdi kongro,
La dang ngangpa angta sa-angni.

Yimrenla – Ratipuklar zoni aishina tsükajentsüko,

Sür ngangpa sako yur;
Sako mana jaruerla,
Niang tsungrem kümertsar,
Diphu yimdongtsü,
Nina tsümeno.

English translation:

Yimoti – In this world we are passersby,

Even if we put on ten enemies head;
Hang the skulls of mithun,
We are like guests,
In the land of the dead in Ayi street;
Meet warriors,
We have battles;
Wife of a warrior,
Tell her to get married.

Yimrenla – In a land where the sun rises from the west,

Whose son keeps trophy's head?
And dance on the top of it,
I wish I become like a god;
Diphu Street,
I want to pass by.

The idea of heaven where the souls enjoy everlasting peace is illustrated by this story and song. This is also another song sung by Yimrenla when she went to tell her mother-in-law about her plan to get married:

Kongro ngangpa odita,
Küjem changzapong tevi jebyatalini;
Senti dangko amongwar shilanglasang,
Ni mengangpa atalidi,
Atali mera,
Kongro ngangpa odini.

English translation:

When I told her I'll get married,
My mother-in-law cried;
One that stays in the land of the dead,
If only you return,
I'll wait for you without marrying;
I waited but you never return,
Let me get married.

Longdangsüja Mongru: There are other songs and stories which talk about life in the land of the dead. Here is a similar story about a couple named Arülepba and Khangchanaro who were married. After Khangchanaro gave birth to two children her husband died. While alive he had told his wife not to re-marry anyone after his death because he will be gone only for a short while and will return soon to unite with her again. She promised her husband and waited for a long time but he never came back. Finally, she decided to send *arasentsür* (soothsayer) to *asüyim* (land of the dead) to know what all was happening in that part of the land and to get some information about her husband. When *arasentsür* met Arülepba in the land of the dead he sent this message through a song. After listening to his song she sang this song:

Arülepba – Akümli yimla tenkalim lima,

Sako tera yokna;
Jongpong sünga yokna,
Bendanger amongra medem,
Kü dangila oro lima ayidemenko;
Par ajurur
Kuaarong mapang khano;
Sarür ejem süngdi kongro,
La dang ngangpa angta sa-angni.
Khangchanaro-Ratipuklar zoni aishina tsükajentsüko,
Sür ngangpa sako yur;
Sako mana jaruerla,
Niang tsüngrem kümertsar,
Diphu yimdongtsü,
Nina tsümeno.

English translation:

Arülepba – In this world, we are just passersby,

Even if we earned fame by bringing ten trophy heads;
Hung the skulls of Mithun *(at our front door house)*
We are equivalent to a guest
Towards my land, in the land of the dead on Ayi street;
I meet other warriors,
We have wars and battles;
Wife of a warrior (addressing his own wife)
Tell her to get married!

Khangchanaro – In a land where the sun rises from the west,

Who keeps trophy heads?
And dance on them,
I wish to I could be like a god;
Then Diphu Street,
I could pass by.

You can see the song is very similar to the one cited by our friend here, only the characters have different names.

At Meyutsungba's place the souls of the dead transform into hawks and visit the living. It is said that if the hawks come and hover over one's roof top, we must spray water for the hawk to drink and fly away; for the hawk may be a departed soul who has wandered back to the land of the living.

Tekatia Imchen: There is a widely held belief that when a person dies his soul departs from the body and turns into *amu* (hawk) and flies away. The Aos believed that the hawks stay in Longkhum village. It is said the hawks of Longkhum village stay in Lazasübo *tenem* (mount of Lazasübo) in Mongzüki (caves of the hawks) in Wokha. Here all the souls of the dead people stay together.

There is a story why the souls of dead persons of Longkhum villagers stay in Lazasübo instead in *asüyim*. As the story says, a young girl in Longkhum village died. Her mother sent her a shawl to the land of the dead. After sometimes, she saw the same shawl which she had put on her daughter hanging in the mount of Lazasübo. Henceforth, the villagers believed that their hawks stay there.

Meyawati Walling: Our ancestors also believed that the souls of the dead live in "Lazasübo". There is a cliff near Longkhum village. When we asked what the reason of naming the place thus was? They said they had been seeing a lady drying her clothes in the sun on the cliff. On the cliff of the rock, there are holes where the *amo* sleeps. Since the *longsü* period (golden period) it was believed that the hawk comes to us three days after a person dies. Some hawks do not come but most of them come to us. Some people have the tiger's spirit. When a person who possesses the tiger spirit dies, the tiger spirit also dies along with the person.

Tekatia Imchen: Yes we do have that belief. Sometimes the soul transforms into a hawk. According to them even if you try to shoot it no one can get a shot at it. That is one form of the soul which is manifested to the people; this should teach a thing or two to the sceptics who doubt the existence of the soul.

Meyawati Walling: The child's hawk will be smaller in size and if it's an old person then the hawk will have fewer feathers and not so beautiful. If the hawk comes and hovers around the house, we give water and say, "Don't trouble much. Please drink this water and go away". After we give the water, the hawk flies away. If the hawk comes and sits on the roof top of our farmhouse and makes noises, it's an indication that one of the family members will die the same year.

Yabangchila Imchen: If a strong person dies, his hawk will be healthy and strong. We have also heard that the soul of the dead person's hawk makes noises but the souls of the living persons' hawks do not make noises. If the hawk makes noises it's an indication that someone will die soon. So, people used to think and wander who is going to die.

Arsashi Jamir: It was believed by the Ao ancestors that for every person, there is a hawk. If the hawk comes to the living and makes noises then it signifies a death in the house within that year itself.

Longdangsüja Mongru: There is also another song sung by the widow of Penduchepchep which talks about life after death. The Aos observe a mourning period of six days for men and five days for women. The widow went to her field on the 8th day of her husband's death, and she saw a hawk on the edge of her field. The hawk began to come everyday to the field and would warm up the field as she worked. One day, the hawk was not there on the tree which made even the tree look very empty. So, she thought to herself perhaps, the hawk (the soul of her late husband) is at a gathering in Meyutsungba's portal and she sang this song.

Külu sabangna,
Mongzü tesen among mera;

Mera cherong ayingchanoa,
Ora Meyutsungba ayu kakasü?
Salang naklube rongsen yimerla.

English translation:

To my field,
New hawk has not come to stay;
This makes my field empty,
Are they having a conference in Meyutsungba's portal?
To earn wealth for celebrations at his portal.

After she sang this song she went to look for the hawk. She found the hawk dead lying upside down. Someone took his life senselessly for we must remember that the Aos never eat any wild birds that have no bruises on their bodies. In grief she buried the hawk and suffered the pain of separation from her husband a second time!

Bendangsashi Longchar: It is said the souls of the dead come and visit the living though they are unseen by the living. It was because of our carelessness that sudden death occurs to human beings. Some people saw the *asüyim* when they go into a trance. We were told that the souls of the dead live in the same way as they had lived on earth. If the souls of the dead visit the living quite often the living would fall sick; that is why they used to keep a mug full of water near the bed. A mug of water is like a river in the eyes of the dead. So, they cannot cross the river to come and visit the living.

Meyawati Walling: In case of sudden death or accident the dead do not go to Meyutsungba's portal. I have heard that there is a big banyan tree. People who die a natural death would fly and sit on top of the tree but in the case of a sudden death due to accident, the dead would not be allowed to fly and sit on top of the tree, but could sit only on the root of the tree. It is known as *motsünglima* or *motsüngki* (land or house of Motsüng).

Ariyongdang Longchar: People who die suddenly or by

accident, were not allowed to enter Meyutsungba's hearth because his hearth was believed to be holy. Such acts were considered *temenen* (evil) and the soul of the dead were allowed to climb Meyutsungba's *temra,* kind of a veranda attached to the main building at the back of his house.

Tekatia Imchen: It was believed that the souls of the dead pay visits to their family members and relatives for a year immediately after death. So, they would keep for the soul a bowl of rice and curry in a corner at home. In the morning, if they found the rice and curry were spilled, it was believed that the soul of the dead had visited them at night and if the rice and curry were not spilled it was believed that the soul of the dead had not visited them. Again, if any of the family members see a dead person in dreams, they keep rice and curry, in case he visits them. After a year, the living seldom see the dead in dreams.

Temsula Ao: I wonder if there is an end to the life of the soul? I have heard people say that sometimes they can become stones, sticks and even caterpillars before they eventually vanish. But they don't die.

Visitor: One hears of different versions about the length of time required to keep the dead body. According to one view the ancestors observed thirty days of *genna* for some people and only seven days for others. Again some report that they kept the dead body on a bamboo platform after which the dead body was thrown away. With the advent of Christianity the dead body was kept for seven days but now it is for three days.

Temsula Ao: Ao *senden* has changed the mourning period into three days.

Tekatia Imchen & Ariyongdang Longchar: It is six days for men and five days for women.

Merazulu Longchar: There is another practice which is only for dead warriors and rich men. The person concerned would tell his relatives before he dies "let my body be dried for six months, a year or three years and then you throw it away". The drying process will take place in the outer room of the house. The dead body would be placed on a bamboo platform and a slow fire will be made below it. For a stipulated period of time they would observe mourning but after the mourning is over, even if the body is to be kept for six months, normal life would go on. This particular rite is observed in the case of warriors and rich men alone and according to their own wish. It could take three to six months, sometimes even a year.

Student: Does the soul of the dead visit the living? Do we feel the presence of the dead in real life?

Yabangchila Imchen: Yes, they do visit us sometimes and speak with us in dreams. The living would ask the soul of the dead why is he/she visiting them. If we shake hands with the soul of the dead, certainly, we are going to die soon.

Meyawati Walling: When we are lying on the bed and in a state of half-sleep they visit us. We cannot see their physical form but can hear the sound of their movements in the house and when they touch utensils and other things. For a year after a person dies, we would never eat all the food that was cooked at home but kept something for the soul of the dead. Whether it is in our dreams or in the real life, if the soul of the dead visits us, we would tell the dead person to eat all the food we have left for him/her. If the soul of the dead visits the family frequently, that family would face a lot of trouble at home. So, in order to stop the dead person from visiting them, they would close the main entrance to the house and put a bamboo jar of water outside while saying the words:"we are separated by water so don't visit us anymore". Once this is done, they would not visit us any more.

Student: Madam since you have lost your own children can you tell us if their souls visit you in dreams and in real life?

Yabangchila Imchen: From time to time they visit us. I dream of them as if I was cuddling them in the way I had cuddled them when they were alive. However, if we dream of them frequently, then we will fall sick.

Guru Sademmeren Longkumer: It is also believed that the soul of the dead stays till the new grains of rice reach home. Therefore, whatever one cooks at home was first offered to the soul. Saying, "This is for you". We act as if the dead man's soul is around all the time.

Visitor: Do the Christians believe that they will go to the same *asüyim* like their ancestors?

Tako Jamir: In Christian religion, it is believed that any person who does good deeds, will get salvation and will go to heaven. Therefore, after we have converted and accepted Christianity we do not follow animism. *Sangsünü* was only in our forefathers' imagination because nobody has ever lived in the land of the dead or come back to the world from the land of the dead. Now almost all the people have converted to Christianity. There are hardly any believers in the older religion. After Dr Clarke brought Christianity to our land, we have left behind animism and converted to Christianity. Christianity preaches that those who believe in God will go to the New Jerusalem (heaven). Christianity also teaches us to live a truthful life in order that our souls would be saved and go to *honyimti* (heaven), where there would be no more tears, sorrow and hunger. We never grow old in heaven. Our ancestors believed that if I have committed adultery, fornication, robbery and were untruthful on earth I would carry the entire burden and take it to Meyutsungba and go to the backyard of Meyutsungba's portal with shame. The truthful ones will go merrily to Meyutsungba with all his glory and honour. Knowing well that he has finished his life's journey on earth, he will go happily to live in Diphu land (land of the dead).

Teacher: The Christian heaven in contrast is a very ideal, platonic kind of heaven where everything is very happy, the same, forgiving, where one will never grow old. But Meyutsungba's portal is a very realistic world.

Satiba Jamir: We are only trying to uncover what had happened in olden days. However what religion we believe in now, we believe only in that.

Tako Jamir: In my Chuchyimlang village during the *medemsanger* and *mejensanger* era, we have abandoned animistic practices. Later, during the middle part of *kosasanger* era, we have revived our culture but rejected the animism. So, we have composed our songs using the same tune but with the Christian meaning. Of course, we cannot put all our thoughts in one song however we have composed this song. Here is the song:

Oh! Aoyimkong tajungnung
Oh! Tsüngrem yimsü nai, Oh Lijaba yimsü tamajung nangentsüokoni
Oh! menang yimsü Poukumer reshikangshia merenakasa
Oh! anüng ali Tsüngrem Yimsü nai lima ramoker.
Oh! Ao Arogo nungi ochishir yimjongkümerdem,
Oh! Israel Tsüngrem telok nanüngdem sotetjangmano.

English translation:

Oh! in the beautiful Ao land.
Oh! the Christian religion has replaced the bad Lijaba religion
Oh! the pioneers of the former religion were threatened and tortured
Oh! God of sky and earth, you have engulfed the land
Oh! let the Ao churches produce truthful leaders and peace maker.
Oh! Israel God let your likeness be born.

Teacher: Through this song and from the *kosasanger* era rejection of animism had started. Animism was considered as tormentor of the people.

All three of them: We shall meet all the Christians in heaven. There is only one Bible.

Teacher: A bit of Christianity and a bit of Ao tradition is practised by the Aos. They have blended both in their culture.

Visitor: Are the dead buried in their traditional attire?

Tako Jamir: Before the advent of Christianity, when someone died in the family we mourned for the dead person and after the mourning period was over, we would put all the clothes out in the courtyard in the sun and also to announce that he/she is no more with us. This ritual was known as *subo apotsü*. This was to show that the dead person had no relation in the world with the living. After this they take the clothes back inside the house. We do not put these things in the coffin. We came naked and go back naked.

Student: We still use some of the things

Meyawati Walling: Suppose a man's belongings became so dear to him while he was alive on earth and he told his wife to put the things he considered precious to himself in his lifetime away in his coffin they would put only those things away which he desired while living.

Satiba Jamir: If we put all his belongings in the coffin then we would have nothing to inherit.

Tako Jamir: His wife would tell the people who come for the funeral service about her husband's last wish before he died. For instance, if he had told her on his death bed to, put his favourite cup in his coffin to take along with him, she must do so. We used to put such things in his coffin.

Teacher: This is the Ao tradition and not the Christian tradition.

Student: There is a fusion of Christianity and animism here.

Meyawati Walling: The day I die, the elders would put a chicken under my armpit in order to meet Motsüngba along with it. We do this even now.

Yabangchila Imchen: By the time the coffin has to be nailed and closed for burial, we would take out the chicken. We would say to the dead person: "Don't feel lonely but take this chicken and rear it in Motsüngba's place". Both the dead person's soul and the chicken's soul go together to his place and live there.

Arenjenba Ozukum: We take out the chicken from under his arm send only his soul.

Student: Is the chicken then buried?

Arenjeba Ozukum: We throw it away in the jungle.

Yabangchila Imchen: It was told that there is a village in the land of the dead where there are only festivities and no pain and suffering. They rear the chicken and live there in the village after death.

Visitor: What about Sobatiyaba?

Tako Jamir: Yesterday I told you about the gods our ancestors worshipped. There are many gods and each god has his own role in different ways. When a child is born, the Sobatiyaba god tells him how long he will live and blesses him. He decides whether the child would live for fifty years, or twenty years, whether the child will become rich, or he will live the life of the poor. This god who controlled the fate of human beings we called him Sobatiyaba Tsüngrem.

Student: We have discussed this earlier, when a child is born, he or she is born with a *tiya* and that *tiya* will determine whether a person will be successful, wealthy, poor or not. Sobatiyba is a god who gives *tiya* to a person, the moment he or she is born.

Visitor: My point for raising this issue here is to find out whether with the coming of Christianity, do they still believe that their destiny/fate is a gift from Sobatiyaba Tsüngrem?

Imtinochet Jamir: With the change and with the coming of Christianity, we replace Sobatiyaba with the Christian idea of God.

Tako Jamir: There were five god-heads worshipped by our ancestors. But now in Christianity there is only one God. We believe that there is only one God and he will give us the final judgement.

Student: Yes of course. But let us for now continue with our discussion. I would ask this question to the elders. How am I going to recognize my near and dear ones when my soul travels to join them in the land of the dead?

Kikasangla Imchen: When my soul travels to the land of the dead, though unseen by the living, my soul retains my former shape. This is how my parents and relatives come to know me. Our stories tell the same thing.

Guru Sademmeren Longkumer: Our great, great grandfathers whom we have not seen nor met on earth are not seen clearly in dreams also. But suppose, someone is nearing his death, then the souls of all his dead relatives will come and visit him.

After the physical body is buried, the soul travels to the land of the dead. The souls of the dead could easily recognize the fresh arrivals: their relatives, husbands, wives, children or grandchildren. They start a new life in the land of the dead very much on the lines of how they had lived on earth.

Guru Sademmeren Longkumer: Since you liked my earliar stories let me tell you another one. This is a story about a loving couple, Tongpangenba and Sangshila who had no children. Unfortunately Tongpangenba, the husband died suddenly one day. While on his deathbed, he told his wife not to re-marry anyone after his death, for he was sure that he was coming back to unite with her after a period of three years. As promised to her husband, Sangshila waited and waited. Years passed but he did not come back. Finally, she decided to send *arasentsür* (soothsayer), to *asüyim* (land of the dead), to know what was happening in that part of the land and to get some information about her husband. When *arasentsür* met Tongpangenba in the land of the dead he sent his wife the following message:

"In this land we are having festivities everyday. Tell my wife that I am not coming back again and do tell her to get married to someone else." The soothsayer came back and reported the exact happenings in the land of the dead. "Are you sure that you met my husband?" she asked. "Well he told me how his wife carries a big scar on her body". Now this she had not told the soothsayer so she was convinced that she had met her husband and rightly recognized him.

Visitor: From all this it follows that its identity is retained by a soul after the death of the body. So it is not the effects of his deeds that give a specific aura which enables the soothsayer identify him but it is his soul which carries the image of the body?

Temsula Ao: Yes the soul is in the image of the body. According to stories available and also in real life incidents, after the soul has travelled to the land of the dead, the old form is retained.

Merazulu Longchar: Let me give you an example of my wife. After she died, I dreamt of her every night and could sense her presence (soul) at home. So, in order to stop her coming home, I consulted *sangmongtsü* (soothsayer), and requested her to go to my wife and tell her not to visit me anymore. When *sangmongtsü* returned from there, she described her looks and her personality exactly to me, and her big birthmark on her face. When she gave her my message, she told *sangmongtsü* that we were soon going to live together and that was the reason for her searching for me. I would have died if *sangmongtsü* had not stopped her. This way I escaped from her. This gives credence to the belief that when a person dies, his already dead near and dear ones come to meet him half-way and there in the land of the dead, they start a new life like the way we live on earth.

Visitor: Is there a separate word for the soul after death when it retains its former bodily form?

Kikasangla Imchen: No. Even in the land of the dead, they will retain their own names. There is no other word for that. It is through the soothsayer, who was a mediator between the dead and the living, we came to know that we retain our own identity and name there in *asüyim*.

Visitor: Almost thirty years ago I learnt from my Ao friend that *asüyim* is believed to be "beyond the river". Now they say it is somewhere in the sky.

Temsula Ao: It was a kind of an imagination that the land of the dead lies beyond the body of water not specified. We call it *Longritsü*. In Greek mythology also there is mention of river *lati* which you have to cross; many cultures have this. Of course, it is not physically verifiable.

Merazulu Longchar: Once we cross this *Longritsü*, we will reach the Diphu land. *Asüyim* and Diphu *lima* are interchangeable words.

Bendangangshi: The soul starts its journey towards the land of the dead after the death of the corporeal body. There are so many versions about the exact location of the land of the dead. According to one version, below the earth there is an underground world where all the souls of dead people go to start a new life there. Still others believed in Diphu *tenem* (mount Diphu) a mountain beyond the Wokha hills. It is said that before climbing mount Diphu the dead person reaches a stream called *Longritsü* (stream of bitterness); there he/she washed his/her hands. Consequently, a transformation takes place and the earthly shapes turn into a pale and thin form. So, he/she weeps bitterly knowing that he/she is dead and feel nostalgic for the loved ones he/she has left behind on earth. Half way to the land of the dead after crossing the *Longritsü*, he/she is greeted by the souls of the dead people who wait for him/her. There is a herb on the bank of the *Longritsü* river called *molunglem süngo*. Once he plucks and smears the *süngo* on his hands all his bitter regrets turn into gladness, after which the soul gladly enters the Diphu *lima* (land of the dead).

Merazulu Longchar: Suppose, someone came to the house and if he turns in the direction of Diphu *lima,* this is occasionally thought to be a sign that he will die after a couple of years. Even he can predict his own death. If asked how he can do so, he might simply say: "Because I am looking towards the Diphu *lima*".

Imtinochet Jamir: Once the dead person reaches the river, he'll wash his hands and his former shape is replaced by a thinner and transparent one. Then he comes to know that he is dead. After which, he will climb the *sentiatang* (cliff) to reach the land. Truthful ones will be with Meyutsungba and the untruthful ones will roam in the thick prickly bushes called *sangsünü*.

Visitor: From where does the concept of the land of the dead as located in the sky originate?

Kikasangla Imchen: This concept of locating the land of the dead in the sky came after Christianity. Locating in the sky is a Christian doctrine.

Visitor: Do the souls differ according to sex?

Kikasangla Imchen: No.

VIII

The Sexes

Visitor: A clarification. According to the origin myth three couples burst out from Longterok. Then there was division of labour between the sexes; yet there was equality of sexes. But the status of women slowly got downgraded. How do the elders perceive this situation? Did they maintain difference in the status, difference in social activities and labour, for men and women in the olden days?

Rongsenwati Longchar: God made man and woman with different natures.

Arenjenba Ozukum: It is said before the Aos came and settled permanently in Chungliyimti women laughed in a different tune called *mongtijilaklak* and men laughed in the *pangsemsemsem* tune.

Tako Jamir: Since the *longsü otsü* (golden age), our forefathers have regarded women as slightly inferior to men. The concept of women will become clearer when we appreciate the roles men and women played during our forefathers' time. To explain their roles we can take the example of a cucumber plant that bears two cucumbers. Of them the smaller one is the female and the bigger one is the male. From this example, the concept of inferiority and superiority (of women and men) has emerged. When it comes to insects like a pair of *süngkok* (grasshoppers) they took the smaller ones as females and the bigger ones as the males.

Kikasangla Imchen: Women were supposed to look after the house and prepare food both at home and in the field.

Teacher: With nature, they were very neutral but when it comes to differentiate men from women they favour men as the superior ones.

Student: Let us ask the question why man is different from woman?

Visitor: Let us first ask the question, do they also have a soul and a mind, besides their body?

Merazulu Longchar: Both men and women have the same body, mind and soul. Our forefathers never thought that women were so different from men because all were regarded as human beings.

Arsashi Jamir: But when it comes to manual work and social status, men have the upper hand.

Teacher: From their size, they derived an understanding that there is difference in capacity.

Tako Jamir: According to our customary law, women were not allowed to participate in decision-making bodies. Only men could participate. Since our forefathers' time, we were told to love women and when we returned home from the battle with injury men expected the women to nurse them. Our parents told us, "Men provide food at home but it was the duty of the women to prepare and serve the food at home". Men did not confide in women on some important matters: If an enemy's village were to be attacked or the men were to go to war they assembled in *arju* and discussed the plan which was not disclosed to women. There was oath taking and a promise made to each other not to disclose the plan to their wives.

Teacher: When men knew that they were physically stronger than women, they clearly separated their function and duty from the women. This led to the division of labour between men and women. When the manual labour was divided, the lighter work was expected to be done by the womenfolk and men took up the heavier and more difficult tasks. But because of their greater physical strength men were expected to be protective of women. This was also the reason why women were assigned lighter duties such as taking care of the chores at home and men took the heavier tasks of going to war, protecting the women and children from enemies, etc.

Meyawati Walling: Women were meant to look after household affairs and they were not used in any village administration. However, in all the festivities both men and women came together and celebrated. But nowadays, because of education women have begun to do men's work. In olden days, there was no education, and women were not allowed to work, for example, in the village administration.

Merazulu Longchar: In olden days, women were regarded as inferior to men unlike in our own times. They were not used for any public and political roles and they were not allowed to perform any rituals and sacrifices. Only after widowhood was woman allowed to offer an egg in her farmhouse. During social functions, their clanswomen were allowed to take part in composing songs and during the harvest season the *patzalar* (clans women) were allowed to sing songs in the farmhouse in order to invoke blessings. (It is said Aos wrote their script on the hide of animal but the dog ate it up, that is why we have no written literature.)

Student: I also learnt from my grandparents that unmarried young women live in *sangsünü* (prickly bushes) after their death. They will struggle in the prickly bushes trying to come out but will not be able to escape from there.

Teacher: Since most educated girls do not want to marry these days, the idea of *sangsünü* has been revived because it is the women who have to procreate for the successive generations.

Visitor: What about unmarried men?

Imtinochet Jamir: This applies to both young unmarried men and women.

Tekatia Imchen: Women were regarded as helpers for men. According to one analogy women were just *teptsüngdi* (side walls).

Arsashi Jamir: In the olden days, in our culture, it was mandatory for the young girl to get married so that she could procreate and the parent's property could be inherited by their offspring. Parents felt disappointed when their daughters were unmarried because they wanted to see their offspring before they die. If they refused to get married, the parents used to tell them that they were going to struggle in prickly bushes on their way to Meyutsungba's portal after death in order to persuade them to get married.

Merazulu Longchar: When it comes to the status of women, no matter how rich her parents are, she cannot inherit or take anything from her parent's side. Once she marries a man, she assumes her husband's status throughout her life.

Yabangchila Imchen: Women were not allowed to inherit any property. Suppose my husband and I have no children, then our property will be inherited by his brothers. If we have male children then they will inherit their father's property. A woman can inherit only her mother's ornaments but man can inherit all the properties at home including his parent's house. This is the reason we say there is nothing to inherit for a woman and we also called women *aningnoza*.

Teacher: This is a term (*aningnoza*) that is used to refer to women and children.

Temsula Ao: In a family they have children, both boys and girls. So, the status of a woman starts from then onwards. Men of course are physically more powerful than women. When and why was the practice of only men inheriting their parent's property introduced? Did it happen at the time of *longterok* or when?

Guru Sademmeren Longkumer: According to legend, man first burst out of the earth at *longterok* that is why man has the upper hand. Culture and longevity are the same for both men and women, that is why when a person dies three days of mourning are observed for both sexes which is the formal period of separation of the living from the dead. But the actual days of mourning for a man is six days and for a woman it is a day less in line with her status.

Meyawati Walling: Since our forefather's time, duties between a man and a woman were clearly demarcated and we have been following the same norms till today. For instance, my wife and I have no children and if I die, she will stay in this house till she dies, when it will be inherited by *tsenmanger*, i.e. my brothers and their male children.

Merazulu Longchar: Women do not inherit any property. However, the wealth they earned together as husband and wife, she can enjoy till his death. Only after his death, she has no rights over the property. Of course, if the husband is willing to gift something to his in-laws he can do so. Division of labour is because she is physically weaker than men, she does her work according to her physical capacity and that is the logic of the division of labour between men and women. She is not allowed to share any power in the village administration which also lowers her status.

Visitor: Is this true for all the different clans?

All of them: Yes.

Student: What about at home? Who has the last word in decision-making at home?

Kikasangla Imchen: Wife's decisions become important at home. A family is considered better if others in the family listen to her and accept her advice. The conversations we have at home with her and her advice is useful even in administrative affairs. No one but a married man can give any of the feasts, including feast of merit, and he must have the wife's consent for this. The wife plays an honourable and conspicuous part throughout. But, of course, as everybody has said, in Ao's culture, women are not allowed to participate in village administration.

Visitor: What ought to be the relation between man and woman? How does tradition describe the duties of man towards woman and woman towards man?

Merazulu Longchar: A woman does the household chores but we don't have specific rules laid down for a woman to be followed nor so for a man. Whatever work we have, we share according to our capacities. In order to have a happy family, woman should be tolerant towards her husband. Apart from weaving, both husband and wife share all the chores. Whatever they produce from their field or earn through other means, it is the wife's duty to share equally with her parents and with her in-laws. It is her responsibility to maintain peace and harmony with her relations.

Guru Sademmeren Longkumer: If they kill a *mithun* (a cow) in the village, along with her *onü* (husband's sisters) she can organize festivities and perform the related rituals. But rituals such as the ones for appeasing gods in times of sickness, fall strictly in the domain of men.

Temsula Ao: In many families there are cases of husband beating and insulting the wife. In such cases, do her relatives and clansmen have the power to protect her?

All of them: Yes.

Husband, Wife and her Protection

Merazulu Longchar: I may want to beat and insult my wife but I have the fear that her relatives and clansmen will take revenge on me and would bring me a bad name in the society. Therefore, I restrain myself from such acts. Yes. Her relatives and clansmen have the right and the power to protect her.

Student: Let me summarize the discussion so far. Except for weaving, which only the women does, there was no clear-cut division of labour between husband and wife. At home, all the major decisions are taken by the wife. Women can participate in festivities related to the rituals but they were not allowed to perform any religious rituals in many occasions. A woman gets protection from her relatives and clansmen if she is physically hurt and mentally tortured by her husband. The punishment would vary depending on the extent of the pain he caused his wife. He will be fined, or even subjected to physical violence by her relatives and clansmen.

Visitor: What ought to be the duty of a man towards his wife?

Merazulu Longchar: My duty towards my wife is to make her happy by doing good deeds for my in-laws, her relatives and also for her.

Guru Sademmeren Longkumer: If he can afford, good husbands buy valuable ornaments for their wives and also make her rest at home when she is pregnant and during early motherhood, respect her and do all the agricultural works. The husband tries to be tolerant towards his wife but when she provokes him by mentioning his parents' name and clan name, that marks the beginning of a serious difference at home which may eventually end in divorce. Whether we are rich or poor, we give nourishing food to our wives especially during early stages of child rearing.

Merazulu Longchar: If we have good harvest in the field and donate 10 per cent of our grains to others, such acts make us happy. After due consultations with the wife, we donate a few good measures of rice to the poor people. This small act of sharing gives us great joy. I am saying this from my own experience.

Visitor: What about men marrying non-Aos? Will an outsider from another community, become an Ao woman after her marriage to an Ao man?

Marriage Between Ao's and Non-Ao's

Tareptsüba: We have a patriarchal society. Suppose I marry a Nepali girl and take her to my village then she will be inducted into the Ao community. Further, she will adopt a person in the village as her father.

Visitor: What about the case of men who marry Ao women? One knows of the example of Natwar Thakkar, who has become a respected member of the Ao community after his marriage to an Ao lady.

Tako Jamir: If a woman marries a non-Ao then she will have to follow her husband's culture. Natwar Thakkar is a social worker who lives in Chuchuyimlang village. When Morarji Desai was the prime minister of India, he visited Chuchuyimlang village and this was through Natwar Takkar's initiative. Even the IGNOU centre of learning and other elite institutions were all set up in Chuchuyimlang village through his initiative. There are up to 40-50 per cent student enrollment in these institutions. The Chuchuyimlang youngsters need not go to far-off places for their studies but can conveniently study in their village itself, which is now a small town. It is a blessing for our people and we owe this to our social worker Natwar Thakkar. He married an Ao lady from Merangkong village and he hails from the state of Gujarat. He first came to Chuchuyimlang in the year 1925. He took many initiatives in order to help the blind and physically disabled people by training them to use their special abilities.

Visitor: Did his wife (Lentinaro) become a Gujarati or does she still retain her identity as an Ao?

Tako Jamir: According to our culture, she should become a Gujarati and should adapt to her husband's culture. In this case, since they have been living and are settled in Chuchuyimlang town post-marriage, she is following her Ao culture. But if they go to Gujarat then she has to become part of Gujarati culture.

Teacher: According to Ao tradition, there are steps to be followed by a non-Ao if he or she marries an Ao. They have to choose a man as their guardian from one of the clans. It could be from a Longchar, Jamir, Walling, Aier, Longkumer, or Pongener clan, etc. Once some one from any of these clans agrees to be the guardian, he assumes the role of a father to him/her. Once the guardianship is accepted, the aspirant for marriage attends and takes part in all social activities.

Student: This procedure is followed even by the Aos. Take for instance, my teacher friend here who hails from Khensa village and I who hail from Süngratsü village: if she marries a man from my village then she too has to follow the same procedure as any outsider would have to. However, it is not mandatory. It depends on the person's choice.

Visitor: Do the Aos expect adherence to all norms, customs and duties from the non-Aos if he/she becomes a part of them after following all these procedures?

Tako Jamir: In the case of Natwar Thakkar, since his wife is from Longkumer clan, he has chosen a man as his guardian from the Jamir clan. So, he has to abide by the rules and regulations of the Chuchuyimlang village council as long as he lives in that village.

Student: Does he contribute *yimsaru* (village local tax or membership fee)?

Tako Jamir: Others have to pay *yimsaru*. Natwar Thakkar requested the village council to exempt him from *yimsaru* because he is only a social worker and the council agreed. The village council's rules and regulations are not rigid but flexible depending on the situation and the person's profession. He has brought all the development to the village, even the State Bank of India. All these activities and initiatives were brought by him because of our mutual understanding with him. He is a good person and doing all the good deeds.

On Love, Marriage and Divorce

Visitor: Let us move on to something which must interest us all, that is the idea of love. What is the Ao word for love? Can it be between husband and wife only or also with others?

Merazulu Longchar: The Ao word for love is *temeim*.

Guru Sademmeren Longkumer: Love is not just between husband and wife and we do love our friends, neighbours and our relations and they reciprocate our love.

Visitor: Is there a special word for the kind of love shared by man and woman?

Kikasangla Imchen: No.

Visitor: Is there any punishment for extra marital relationships? This is important because from here we will come to know how sacred the bond of marriage is.

Merazulu Longchar: If any one of the couple has an extra marital affair, then the wrongdoer was fined four to five pigs known as *kilamet*. Suppose my wife has an extra marital affair, then both my wife and her lover would be fined and punished.

Student: What was the marriage system like in olden days?

Merazulu Longchar: In olden days, marriages used to take place during the Tsüngremmong festival with a formal meeting between both the families and relatives. Once the couple got the approval from both sides they sanctified the house by tying an egg on the front pillar of the house. However if a baby was born to them before ten months of their marriage, that child was not included as a member in the village councils when he became an adult.

Guru Sademmeren Longkumer: *Larlapong* is a word for the children of a man and a woman belonging to the same clan. These children were prohibited from any resposibility in social and political administration. *Ketachir* means children born out of wedlock. Since Chungliyimti's times, they too were not used in any village administration.

Merazulu Longchar: If a man marries a woman within the same clan, they were sent out of the village.

Visitor: What about divorce?

Kikasangla Imchen: Divorce was prevalent in olden days too. Even after we got divorced, we used to go and attend to the first wife or husband's funeral house till his or her death and observe the mourning period. After a couple is divorced, and if they still love each other they are considered as destined to be together. They were accepted as husband and wife like before.

Merazulu Longchar: If divorce happens through mutual understanding there was no fine and punishment. Their wealth and properties were equally divided.

Guru Sademmeren Longkumer: If a married man wants to marry another woman by divorcing his wife, he will leave his present house and will take with him only his spear and plate. Their present house will be given to his first wife. Similarly, if a married woman wants to marry another man by divorcing her husband, she too will be allowed to take only her personal belongings. Although Aos do not have any written laws, their laws are as powerful as any written laws. We follow our customary laws even today.

Yabangchila Imchen: Whoever is right will have the last word in case of divorce. No household belongings will be given to the person who wants the divorce.

Meyawati Walling: In olden days, every year we used to cultivate the fields. The field which was cultivated the previous year (*meyaphu*) was cultivated the next year as well along with the new field (*lothi*) of that year. So, we cultivated two fields in a year. We used to have separate granaries for storing the grains. The grain from the *manenthi* granary (a grain similar to wheat) will be given to the wife whether they have more or less grain. The grain from the other granary will be given to the husband. Suppose, the wife was found guilty then she will take only her clothes and the *manenthi*.

Visitor: Can the church give them permission to divorce independently of the village council?

Both of them: Church never gives its approval for separation. Even the relatives do not want them to separate because they think that by this act, they are committing a sin against God. Whoever is in the wrong, his membership will be removed from the Church and the Church will never give him a second chance to re-marry in the Church. But the other person who was not in the wrong can re-marry in the Church.

Visitor: It means that the community laws are strictly adhered to.

Student: But there are cases of the second wife staying in her late husband's house after his death. How is this allowed if as per Ao law, only sons inherit the house and properties of the dead man?

Tareptsüba: If there is mutual understanding amongst them the son can let his step-mother stay in his father's house. For this, no decision of the village council is necessary.

Merazulu Longchar: If there is some misunderstanding between them over the properties then the village council will decide their case. If not, the children can take care of their step-mother and her children. The second wife and her children are not abandoned at all.

Guru Sademmeren Longkumer: If the new wife behaves well they can help each other in every possible way; but if she misbehaves and has affairs with other men then they will chase her out of the house. The children from the first wife will take over the house.

It is the responsibility of the elder brothers to take full custody of the children from the second wife.

IX

Strangers in Ao Country

Visitor: Dear sirs, when I entered the village the people referred to me as *bendanger*, which, I presume, means a stranger. Can we also use the same word for visitors who are Nagas from other clans or generally people you don't know personally?

Tareptsüba: *Bendanger* refers only to persons who are total strangers. A fellow villager even if not known personally can not be called *bendanger*. The village council will fine anyone who uses the word *bendanger* for a person who belongs to the same village. Strangers such as you who come to the village with good intentions are welcome. For it is possible that he may turn out to be your *temba*, meaning best of friends.

Merazulu Longchar: *Temba* is a term meaning friendship between two persons belonging to different clans within a village or with persons from other villages. If they are very close they are known as *tembaji*. Then, even if they belong to different villages, whoever dies first, the living one will observe the mourning period of six days. There is no blood tie with *tembaji* but by their good deeds to each other they become just as close. They share all their sorrows and happiness together. *Tinu* is also a similar kind of friendship.

Student: Aos are not necessarily hostile to strangers. Just like their ancestors, they would attack a stranger only when the outsider or stranger tries to threaten them and take away their belongings.

Visitor: So the appearance of strangers in our midst does not necessarily imply that they are enemies. But there was tension and wars between Aos and other communities?

Merazulu Longchar: Inter-community conflicts and wars happen when a person kills another who hails from a different village without a good reason. For such senseless killings the village was bound to attack the village of the killer. For in olden days, it was incumbent on them to take revenge; not to do so would be shameful and the villagers would be regarded as characterless.

Guru Sademmeren Longkumer: I know of the case of a stranger who belonged to the Longchar clan who was allowed by the village council to stay in with a Longchar family for he was a man of good character. Others who entered the village with bad intention were sent off. However this practice has now stopped. Under British administration, outsiders were required to take permission to stay from the sub-divisional office.

Merazulu Longchar: After British administration was established, all disputes within the village or between two villages that could not be resolved by the village councils were taken up to the sub-divisional office. But some cases relating to strangers continued to be settled by the village council itself.

Student: Suppose, a stranger still wants to enter the village even after he was sent off. Who has the last word, the stranger or the village council?

Arsashi Jamir: Even if he was permitted to stay in the village by the sub-divisional officer the village council's decision is final.

Teacher: We differentiate tribals from non-tribals. All the non-tribals are called *tsümar*.

Bendanger is a term used not only for non-Aos or non-tribals but it is used for Aos as well. The term *bendanger* is a very general term. We also use the words, *ayenger yimako* meaning in a stranger's village. If we do not have blood relation with a person we may call him *bendanger*.

Arsashi Jamir: In Chungli dialect we call strangers *bendanger* and the word in Mongsen dialect is *rasemer*. An outsider or stranger could be from your own village or from another village and also from your own village with whom you have no blood relation.

Student: They have not categorized non-tribals as *tsümar*. In general, they call all outsiders *bendanger* irrespective of whether they are tribal or non-tribal.

Teacher: *Tsü* means water. *Mar* means over the water. Please remember that there is Brahmaputra on one side. Our immediate neighbour is Assam, hence the connection with the others.

Student: In short, for the Aos stranger means *bendanger*. We understand from the discussion that they used two terms for strangers. *Tsümar* for the non-tribal, and *bendanger*, a stranger from within the same village or from another village. Non-Aos like Konyaks can be called *bendanger* and not *tsümar*. Any Naga who is a stranger to the Aos is called *bendanger*. The Aos only called non-tribals *tsümar*. The other Naga tribes may have their own term.

Tako Jamir: Suppose, some people from other states come to Mokokchung then we call them *tsümar* but if some Nagas like the Lothas, Angamis, Chakesang come to Mokokchung then we called them *bendanger*.

Student: What they are saying is that strangers within Nagaland are called *bendanger* and if any strangers come from outside Nagaland they are called *tsümar*. They can tell from his features whether a person is a Naga or not.

Visitor: Is there inter-marriage between the Aos and the *tsümar*?

Tako Jamir: Our socio-cultural life was very different from theirs. Therefore, our forefathers considered inter-marriage with *tsümar* a taboo.

Visitor: There are stories about an Ahom king marrying an Ao princess.

Tako Jamir: This inter-marriage between the Ahom king and the Ao princess happened later. It happened when our culture was evolving. The king's wife hailed from Nokrang village. She was the daughter of the village headman. For the bride price, the headman of Nokrang asked the Ahom king for a hornbill that has got two black stripes on its feathers. Usually, hornbills have only one black stripe. The Ahom king painted a second stripe on the hornbill and gave it as the bride price. While that bird was flying in search of fruit to eat, it was caught and trapped in a *mezapang* (an instrument to trap birds) in the forest of Longkhum village. After the bird was trapped, Ajangrongpang and Jaksüngnaro, plucked the bird's feathers and decided to sell it outside the Ao territory and with a higher price in order to show to others that in Longkhum village, there were hornbills with uncommon feathers. As they roamed from place to place looking for a customer, they happened to come into Nokrang village. On seeing the bird's feather, the headman of the Nokrang village who was the father-in-law of the Ahom king thought that the Longkhum villagers have killed the bird which was the bride price for his daughter and killed the sellers. Later, there was enmity between these two villages. There is a book titled *Stories of Penduchepchep*. This book has this story.

Imtinochet Jamir: Yes, the Ahom king married the Ao woman; but it happened in relatively recent times. Since inter-marriage with *tsümar* was considered a taboo it was strictly observed by our forefathers in the olden times. The Nokrang headman thought that by demanding a bride price which he knew the Ahom king could not possibly pay, he would prevent the marriage. But he was tricked by the king, who painted a second stripe on the bird's feathers. Thus the marriage did take place.

P. Ato. Jamir: Since he was reluctant to marry off his daughter to a *tsümar,* he demanded an impossible thing as bride price.

Teacher: Since the king fulfilled the headman's demand, he gave his daughter in marriage to the Ahom king. Here only *ochiba* (truthfulness, honesty) mattered. It took precedence over his wish.

Visitor: Within their own community the Ao standards of morality are very strict. Are they equally strict in relation to persons other than Aos.

Student: Their contact or interaction with *tsümar* was not so frequent but they had trade with them – that is clear. So, what kind of ethical standards were in place in trade relations of Aos with *tsümar*?

Meyawati Walling: *Tsümar*s, as has been informed, did not visit Ao villages frequently in olden days. We had visitors from other Ao villages. Whosoever Aos came to us we called them *aener*. The only condition was that if you belonged to the Longchar clan when you visit us, you should go to a house owned by someone who also belongs to the Longchar clan. Suppose we are observing *amou* and a friend of ours from another village visits us, we would tell him to sleep in someone else's house for that night and only the next day will we allow him to come home.

Tako Jamir: One person from my village had made good friendship with the Ahom king. So, the king of Ahoms gifted him a pair of shoes made of metal. We Aos are hospitable to outsiders whether *tsümar* or any other. The Aos may lack in other fields of knowledge but we have an extraordinary gift: an instinct to observe and understand other people's way of life and nature. In one meeting, we could easily understand a person's nature whether he is a good or bad person. In short, our ancestors did not have daily contact with *tsümar* but whenever they met them for trading purposes or on any other occasions, they tried to be good to them and make friendship.

Visitor: Is *temba* (good friendship) possible with *tsümar*?

Teacher: Yes, *temba* was made with *tsümar*. There was friendship between the king of Ahoms and Pangjunglemba from Chuchuyimlang village. It was not a treaty but friendship.

Visitor: Can the *temenen* (bad force) attack *tsümar*, *bendanger*, and non-Aos?

P. Ato. Jamir: Human beings have *tiya* but it is relative to a situation. For instance, I may have a weak *tiya* today and at other times I may have a strong *tiya*. On a day when an outsider has a weak *tiya*, irrespective of whether he is tribal, non-tribal or *tsümar*, *temenen* will attack him. Therefore, it applies to all.

Visitor: Can a *tsümar* and *bendanger* go to the land of the dead?

P. Ato. Jamir: In olden days, had there been many religions like Christianity, Hinduism and Islam as we have come to know in modern times, then, they might have thought something more about it. But in olden days, they never thought beyond their own religion.

Visitor: Can a stranger who comes and stays in the village and brings fame and honour for the village (such as Natwar Thakkar), be entitled to be a *nokinketer*, an exceptional man?

Yabangchila Imchen: He was entitled to be a *nokinketer*. The villagers will compose songs in his honour. He was treated as equal with the rest of the villagers. The quality of life led is more important than the membership of a group. *Nokinketer* is known for his actions, of courage and valour and not just as a member of a group.

Kikasangla Imchen: *Nokinketer*s were the leaders and smart people in the society.

Student: But then who is a *walunir*?

Guru Sademmeren Longkumer: *Walunir* is a multi-talented person. He is a wise person, a good leader, a good administrator and a good warrior.

Merazulu Longchar: He was the one who gave feast to the villagers by killing *mithuns*. He was a good and hard-working person. *Süsabuk* means a promise made by a warrior to sacrifice his life for the cause of his people in the battlefield. That is what the *Nokinketer* did. His rank was equivalent to a general in the army.

Kikasangla Imchen: The Ao ancestors won many battles in the war with others. Perhaps, this concept of *walunir* was the outcome of the victory in the battles during war.

The Walunir and the Nokinketer

Visitor: But then what is the difference between a *nokinketer* and a *walunir*? *Nokinketer* too sacrifices his life for the people in war time, does he not?

Merazulu Longchar: *Walunir* is a person who sacrificed his life for the people in warfare and also gave feasts to the villagers by killing *mithuns* while a *nokinketer* sacrifices his life for the people in war but does not kill *mithuns* to give feasts to the villagers. A count of *mithun* heads shows how hard-working a *walunir* was. A *nokinketer* is only a warrior but a *walunir* is an all-rounder. However both are praiseworthy. The village folk will compose songs for both of them in praise of their good deeds. *Nokinketer* songs will speak about his valour, actions, sacrifices and how many heads he has brought, etc. *Walunir* songs will speak about how many *mithuns* he killed for feasting his villagers, his leadership quality, his sacrifices in the battlefield etc.

Rongsenwati Longchar: One who brought trophy heads for the villagers was a *nokinketer*. They believed that a warrior was appointed by Yimkong Tsüngrem (god of all) and Yongpang Tsüngrem (river god). Becoming a *nokinketer* is a gift of god. Young boys pierced their earlobe and put cotton roll the day a *nokinketer* brought trophy heads to the village *yimrong* (a place where trophy heads are kept). There were also people who killed *mithun* and fed the villagers but *nokinketer* was respected more in the society because he protected the villagers from their enemies. *Walunir* was a person who was good in public administration and also a trusted leader.

Student: While travelling through the Ao villages, we have been shown a few of the places (*yimrong*), where they lay the trophy heads brought to the villages by the warriors. We were told that the entire village would gather together at the *yimrong* and dance singing praises of the warriors who brought the trophy heads.

Repjensangba Longchar: A warrior was honoured and

respected so much in the society. They exalted his name, songs were composed in his name and they thought him stronger than elephants and tigers. *Nokinketer* was respected more in the society than a *walunir*. Suppose, they had an argument, *nokinketer* always won the argument with these words, "don't argue with me, you are surviving because I protect you from the enemies". This song was composed for Pangerchiba who was a warrior:

Ningjangpangko tsümok atentatsü,
Atsü tsümok nongna,
Noksenkokba teba jangchen.

English translation

There are thunders in the sky,
No this is not thunder
It is the vibrating presence of Pangerchiba.

Merazulu Longchar: *Nokinketer* never thought of his well-being but sacrificed his life for the people. Once a *nokinketer* brought a trophy head, the victim happened to be his girlfriend a rich and a beautiful girl from Mongchen village, whom he came to know when he went for head hunting to Lakhu and Lirmen villages. The day he went to invade Mongchen village he tried his level best to let his girlfriend escape from her enemies so he let her hide in granary but his efforts failed. He knew that she'll be killed by his friends so he killed her instead. He brought the trophy head along with her necklace and handed them over to the village elders but they did not return him the necklace. So, out of anger his wife said to the villagers, "you are surviving because of my husband". The village *patir* (elders) fined her a pig. Her husband ran away from the village because of this incident but later on he was called back. In those times, it was taboo to talk about your own achievements.

One who sacrifices his life in the battlefield for his people and brought trophy heads for the villagers was called a *nokinketer*. He led the villagers to war and guarded them till the battle was over.

Suppose there were no *nokinketer* in the village then all the men would assemble and promise themselves that they will sacrifice their lives for the people (*süsabok*). There is a saying which goes: "whenever *nokinketer* stamps on the ground, it shakes the sky!" He was respected and honoured as god by the villagers.

Tekatia Imchen: After death his soul enjoyed eternal bliss. Under Meyutsungba's care his life will be full of happiness and festivities.

Longdangsüja Mongru: Once upon a time, there lived a wealthy man named Sao in Chungliyimti (the first Ao village settlement). After his death his soul was tested by Meyutsungba. It is said Sao went to Meyutsungba's portal in a very proud and boastful manner thinking all his fame and wealth was earned by himself alone and wanting to show off. Sao never realized that he was blessed by Meyutsungba. Sao very arrogantly told Meyutsungba that he had come to warm up his portal. So, Meyutsungba replied "There are thousands of people to warm up my portal, go back to the world and unite with your wife. Even the jungle plant *sürawa* (*latania*) has not grown enough yet to make your coffin." In olden days, dead bodies were wrapped in with the bark of a plant that grows in the forest. In order to teach him a lesson Meyutsungba sent him back to the world for a second life. This is a song sung alternately by Sao and Meyutsungba.

Sao – Oro Meyutsungba o,

Nü kima lemlemve,

Nika larayatar.
Meyutsungba- Kü kima lemlemvila,

Meyeyar-er rokra lanoa,
Nang koa-er nü jemer den yongyemjokang;
Na lep tsapela,
Ongjang süra memelongona.

English translation:

Sao – Oh! Meyutsungba,

To warm up your portal,
I have come.

Meyutsungba – My compound is warm enough,

There are thousands of people,
Go back to the world and unite with your wife;
To make your coffin,
Even the Latania plant hasn't grown enough yet.

Bendangangshi: The second time around in this world Asemchiba had a very hard and poor life. Meyutsungba took back all his wealth and fame because Asemchiba never realized all his fame and wealth were from his creator. After his death when he went to Meyutsungba's portal he had nothing to offer him. Asemchiba said to Meyutsungba, "I have brought only a small bird sent by my *arjununger*, friends in dormitory, I am sorry to say". Do you know what was the response of Meyutsungba to this? Meyutsungba said, "My dear fellow that too was actually from me".

Guru Sademmeren Longkumer: In order to earn fame and honour in the society rich families gave feasts to the entire villagers by killing a *mithun*. Before they go to Sema areas to buy *mithuns* they husk the rice. On that day, they hoist an egg basket with an egg wrapped in clean *amwa* (banana leaf) in the fork of a tree. Young girls in the colony and their *ilangtsür* (clan-women) helped the family with the husking. Aos never reared *mithuns*; they bought them from tribes such as the Mongtirs and Semas in the months of April and May.

Süachiba was regarded as the highest form of worship to *Tiyar Tanüla* (god of destiny). That day the rich man's best friends, clan-women and his peer group will compose songs in praise of him and the warriors will also come and dance in his house. For the second time too, they have to offer *mithuns* in sacrifice. The wife used to adorn her hair bun with an *ozümi* (hornbill feathers) and the husband will put three *ozümi* (bird feathers) in her bun. Depending on the number of *mithuns* killed, the number of *ozümi* would multiply.

Kikasangla Imchen: The rich men in our forefathers' time had to perform certain actions and rites while announcing their wealth. First, they had to kill three pigs. Second, on the day of the feast, they were expected to have huge amounts of meat in the house. All his relatives had to donate pigs. They killed almost ten pigs. Third, they would decorate their shawl with *sangshi* (special beads used to make necklaces) and ornamental bells. Only after all this has been done that the *sangshi* can be ceremonially worn. Although the use of *sangshi* has become common now, in olden days, we never wore *sangshi* without fulfilling all the norms and procedures.

Guru Sademmeren Longkumer: A warrior was respected more by the people than a *süachir* (person who can kill *mithuns*) because the warrior guards and protects everyone from their enemies, so that they could cultivate land and earn more wealth. *Nashiachiba* (cow or bull sacrifice) was performed at home but *süachiba* (*mithun* sacrifice) was performed in Aonglenden, a place in Ungma village where only Aos lived. The day they kill a *mithun*, the sacrificing couple in full attire will perform *Süwalok* (worship of *mithun*) and say these words, one after the other. "After my grandfather and my father made offerings to you in the past, today, I am offering you." The wife should mention her *onülanunger* (father's sister) many times during the act of worship. *Mithun* sacrifice was done in the month of October every year and they kept themselves physically clean on those days.

Merazulu Longchar: One thing we should not forget to emphasize is that both the wealthy and the warriors were persons of great character. Enemies withdrew from the battlefield because they find the force of truthfulness in them, they are not just good men *wapong tajung* and good women *watsü tajung*. Only the truthful ones can achieve such a great honour.

X

Communicating with Nature

Visitor: What about the ability to communicate with nature? I have been told that animals and plants belonged to a lower order than humans, they don't have souls whereas man has soul. But tradition also states that just as there is a possibility of communicating with God so there is a possibility of communicating with animals and plants. So how is this possible?

Guru Sademmeren Longkumer: We do not make friendships, such as *temba* and *tenu*, with trees, plants, animals, rivers and mountains as we do with human beings. But when we perform rituals we may make friends with them.

Temsula Ao: Let me refer here to *lupok* (Mongsen dialect) and *poyok* (Chungli dialect) the name of a system followed in shifting or jhum cultivation which illustrates the camadiere between them. The Ao ancestors kept a gap of ten years for each plot of land for jhum cultivation. For instance, if they cultivate a particular plot of land for two consecutive years, it was abandoned for the next ten years. After completing its ten-year cycle, they will go and cultivate the same land; this is known as *lupok* in Mongsen dialect and *poyok* in Chungli dialect. Once again after two years of cultivating this plot of land, they will switch over to another plot of land that has completed its ten years of lying fallow. So, the ten-year cycle continues.

Now to the ritual part of this exercise. Before the fields are slashed and burnt, the Ao ancestors appease the field god by offering an egg. Then, the second ritual followed after the fields are slashed and burnt. In the second ritual, they offer a cock in order to sanctify the place and to ward off the evil forces so as to avoid injury while working in the field. Then, after the grains sprout they invoke blessings by offering a pig asking for good harvest from the field god.

Student: Yes prior to cultivating a particular plot of land, a pig or a cock is offered to the land. Only after the offering has been made that the slashing and burning take place. This may be regarded as one form of communication between man and nature.

Rongsenwati Longchar: In olden days, when a village was founded, plots of land were divided among different clansmen who formed the village administration. While cultivating the fields they quickly demarcated the village boundaries. The log drum was brought out to signal any emergent situation. If a person was late by one day after the village was founded he was called *tayimer*.

Teacher: One should here recall the *sabang* – the empty space maintained between the borders of the field and the jungle. This speaks of the farsightedness of the ancients who insisted on keeping the empty space as a security measure from both the wild animals and also neighbouring enemies.

Rongsenwati Longchar: There were two types of fields, the land inherited from the forefathers' *aienlu* and the other, the field which was bought by their grandfathers with money or grains, from others. To the former they used to say the following, as preparations for cultivation began: "Ah ha ha I am cultivating this same field, a field worshipped by my grandfathers before me and they had offered you dogs to appease you". To the latter, they said these words: "Ah ha ha I am cultivating the field bought by my grandfathers with their own money and grains, so please help us with your blessings".

Visitor: The humans definitely wish to appease or make friends with the field god. What about the field god? Is there a two-way communication between them?

Tareptsüba: The field god in turn showers his blessings on the cultivator. Let me clarify. They worshipped stones, rivers, mountains, *demen* (road), *kimong* (house) and *yimkülem* (village), etc. because these things provide all their necessities in life. They worshipped water because it cleanses them from all their sins and stones were worshipped because they believed that stone gives them good luck and blessing. *Süngdonglidong* (trees and plants) were worshipped because they provided them with shelters; log drum similarly was hewn out of a huge single log, part of which may be used to make coffins or simply as firewood. They worshipped *kimong* in order to propitiate him so that the new household is blessed with good health and prosperity. The killing of *mithun*s in the village, giving feast to all the villagers was a sign of prosperity. They thought that they were blessed by God if they could rear domesticated animals. They observed seven days *genna* to be physically clean. If any animal died they wrapped rice and salt in banana leaves and tied it to a tree to show their last respect and to ensure that the curse of the dead animal did not fall upon them. If chicks were hatched they never cooked fish at home believing that all the chicks will die. They also observed *genna* for three days for the new born chicks. If pigs gave birth to piglets they observed *genna* for seven days and no visitors were allowed inside the house. Even today, Aos never watch in groups while the pig is giving birth for fear that all the piglets will die. In olden days, they worshipped the *athi* (granary).

Tareptsüba: So also they revered Sobatiyaba who was referred to as *Ita-anü Tsüngrem* (moon-sun god). Moon and sun give light to mankind. They believed that all the natural things such as plants, rocks, mountains and marsh-land have force and can influence human events. They worshipped them along with a host of gods. As they all signify one and the same reality. Of the Ao pantheon, it is Lijaba and Meyutsungba who were the most powerful.

Student: No doubt communication with nature is possible but it can't be like man to man. The first stage of communication was to appease the field god and the second was to sanctify the workplace in order to ward off the evil forces in the field and the third was to invoke blessings for good harvest in the field.

Kikasangla Imchen: We used to select any land for agriculture except the land where tigers killed human beings. *Yimli* (the entitlement due to a community who owned the land) was preserved without cutting down the plants and trees.

Visitor: The invoking and seeking blessings from land (*ali*) give us another insight into the traditional vision of the world. Traditionally the Aos thought of nature as higher than man, definitely not as inferior. Man is not being seen as the centre of the universe.

Temsula Ao: No. In the traditional world-view, man was certainly not the centre of the universe. There were powers above him; those powers resided in the forest, rivers and mountains and also in the land itself. The land is so very important.

Kikasangla Imchen: If we cultivate a plot of land, we offer three piglets in a year. The Christian people make fun of us when we eat the piglets that were offered to the gods. Yes, we ate the meat of the piglets because we do not want to throw away food, besides it is food touched by God himself. We make small pieces of meat and first of all offer them to the gods by putting the meat on small bits of banana leaf. We hoist small sticks near our farm house and put six pieces of meat in every stick. It was later eaten by the wild birds and animals. We also worshipped the god *Kitzüng* at home. We kill the pigs while worshipping *Kitzüng* at home and offered pieces of it to *Kitzüng*. We worshipped *Kitzüng* seeking protection from him from illness and we offered the small pieces of meat at the foot of the main post of the house. In the next morning, we threw away the offered meat.

Visitor: What is the Ao word for nature?

Imtinochet Jamir: *Meta-ayong* which means "anything that surrounds us".

Ariyongdang Longchar: Everything in nature is important

because we need all the things given by nature: water for survival and plants to use for different purposes.

Sashimeren Walling: Wind is considered more important in nature because the wind brings seeds from different places; they sprout and grow into a variety of plants.

Longdangsüja Mongru: It is said Aos lived in a place called *Lakhulepok* **lima** before they permanently settled down in Chungliyimti (the first Ao village settlement). In that land, there was no sun for six months of the year. Half of the year they lived in darkness. Then they measured time by chopping a *yarang* (a variety of banana tree) and the time of its fresh sprouting.

Tekatia Imchen: If there was a sudden storm which caused destruction by uprooting of trees, landslides and sweeping away entire houses, they observed *amou* (*genna*) for a day. On that day, the entire village will have a feast and offer sacrifices to the God by killing pigs.

It was also believed that land was truthful so we were told not to covet even an inch that belonged to another. When there was a dispute between two people over a plot of land, the loser would say the following words, "Please don't have bad feelings towards your grandfather for not winning the case, feel free to cross my land". Only then would he return home.

Korakaba Jamir: We all know that water is the most important thing in nature because it sustains our life. In olden days, human beings used to communicate with nature. They communicated with thunders and storms. Once *kivolong* and *longkerak* wind almost destroyed the *reju* (dormitory) so they built a *ritu reju* and requested the wind to destroy it instead. The wind obliged the village and destroyed the *ritu reju*.

Tareptsüba: There are many stories that speak of the communication between man and nature. Without windstorm, if a tree falls down suddenly on our way, it was believed that a good person would die in the family. If *pentsü* bird chirps, *jongrek jongrek,* it was considered a blessing and if *diphu pentsü* chirps *phe phe* it was considered a sign of misfortune.

Longrimongba Mongru: Between Longkhum and Mangmetong villages there is a river called Tsümajem, which is considered sacred. There is no sacred forests but in deep inside forests they selected big trees called *chuti* for worship and no one was allowed to cut such trees. They could, however, cut trees from the surrounding areas.

Meyawati Walling: The Mangmetong forest was regarded as sacred in olden days known as *alangmezen*. This forest was kept as sacred for so many eras and was the biggest forest in our area but now they have cut down all the trees and there is no forest any more. Those days, hornbills came and built their homes there but everything has gone now. Nothing remains.

Yabangchila Imchen: There is also another forest in our village which was regarded as sacred known as *osakneongmezen*. But again all the trees are cut down now. These two forests were the well-known forests in our territory in olden days.

Rongsenwati Longchar: All the things in nature were considered important because they served us in many different ways and this was considered a blessing. Therefore, they worshipped all the natural things and offered pigs and hens to God. Agriculture was regarded as the most important activity that needed the cooperation of nature.

Imtinochet Jamir: The products of nature are the gift of God to human beings for their daily needs. Water, air, trees and agriculture are necessary for our survival. It is like a combination of different chemicals from which medicines are made for different diseases. Soil is very important for different kinds of seedlings and plants. There are different seasons to sow seeds called *tsüngküm mungpu*. Our ancestors were very careful in doing things. They never took the seeds from other families especially if that family had mad children at home or thieves, etc. According to the position of the moon, they sowed their seeds. The 3rd, 5th, 7th and 9th days of the month were regarded as the best days for sowing seeds in the fields. After the sowing season was over, they invoked the blessings from the field god with these words: *azatsüla ali tebokbana waiokvang, amatsüla kenvokrong, atsüngrongtsü mekongvokchuka molutsüko tezüng yanger mevovang* (let these weeds go downwards below the earth, uproot all the waste and let the seeds sprout out, rooted in *motsü*). Aos celebrate Moatsümong (*moatsü* festival) in order to invoke blessings from God Lijaba by offering pigs and cocks. Along with the performance of all these rituals, they also worked hard in the field to have a good harvest that you must not forget.

Bendangsashi Longchar: After a person died, his dead body, it was believed, turns into a tree which the Aos called *amtong*. It is said *amtong* used to speak to human beings. Long time ago, in the first Ao settlement at Chungliyimti there lived a beautiful girl named Sangrojungla. One morning, she went to the stream to fetch water and was freshening up murmuring to herself *tsüsenjoker, tsüsenjoker* (let me be refreshed, let me be refreshed). A big tree that stood by the bank of the stream responded to her through a song.

Lazati: Tsüsenjoker, Tsüsenjoker
süngdong: Laza süremsüpang,
Yongmen mezortsü,
Teyongtsüko tsüsenjokang.

English translation:

Girl: Let me be refreshed, let me bathe
Tree: Young lady,
The one cleaning the brass ring,
Refresh yourself in the middle of the stream.

On returning home, she informed the village councils what had happened and they resolved to cut down the tree. The villagers proceeded to axe down the tree but they failed. The tree stood firmly as before. So, the villagers returned home without fulfilling their plan thinking the wind would blow the tree down at night. Sentries were sent to find out but they were told that the tree remained firmly rooted to the ground. On the second day, when the villagers went to cut down the tree they were astonished to see the dao-belt (traditional belt worn by the Ao males), tied around the tree which was found to have been gifted by the girl. They realized that the girl's lover was actually a tree who transformed himself into a human being at night. Finally, when the Lemtur clan went to cut the tree, a chip of the tree trunk pierced the girl's eyes and she died on the spot. At the same moment, the tree too crashed down to the ground. Since they could not remove the tree from its place they decided to cut the branches. Suddenly, a windstorm covered its trunk with leaves and the villagers returned home. The Lemtur clan was thenceforth known as *kentonglener* (ones who cut down the singing tree). It is said that if the Lemtur clan sows seeds near a tree the yield multiplies several fold.

Imtinochet Jamir: Many Ao villages maintained reserved forests. They never cut down the trees in the reserved forest except to build *arju* and for the village log drum: within the village, log drum was used for many purposes in order to convey messages to the villagers, to make the entrance and exit gates of the village, and to make coffins for children and the widows. Children and widows were considered physically weaker than the rest of the people in the society. Therefore, the community provided whatever was needed for the last rites for dead children and widows. Their coffins could be made from wood from the trees of the reserved forest. It was shameful to ask for trees for selfish purposes such as to build their own homes, farmhouses, pig-sties, etc. It was also considered generally shameful on the part of an individual to ask for things that belong to the community for his own personal use.

Rongsenwati Longchar: Sentries were posted to guard the log drum and they had the task of beating the drum at times of emergencies. There are different sounds and rhythms of the log drum; from these people could make out whether it was danger that was being signalled or festivities. One of the most important use of the log drum was to signal people to assemble in the *arjukima* (dormitory compound) to go to war. A Longchar team from Ao tribe went to meet Khemungan tribe in order to find out the type of wood they used for making the log drum. They were told that like the Aos, they used *arisüng* to make the log drum. However before they cut down the tree they would go to the area where the tree had grown and say these words:

> Oh handsome river tree, instead of letting the windstorm and landslide uproot you or let passersby trample on you or let the mushroom grow wild on you, do come and guard my village, you will be honoured as we drag you along the way, don't feel bad and humiliated, do come to the village.

In olden days, if they would not take the dead body from the battlefield; they would cut down the *lochetsüng* (name of a tree) and carry it pretending that it was the dead body. In some years, the sap oozed out from this tree. Once I was walking in the streets of Tongmeyu village in the month of March–April. I saw water oozing out of a *lochetsüng* stem and leaves, and there was water all over. So, I asked the villagers what happened to that tree. They replied "the tree was crying"!

Tako Jamir: I think that our forefathers worshipped all the big stones and trees because they believed that there was *mojing* (evil) or a bad force in those trees and stones. When they would go and worship the big trees and stones, the Pongener clan will lead the people. If they go to worship at the *awatsüng* (a lake) the Jamir clan will lead the people.

Teacher: I disagree. It is the being of nature that they worshipped. The character or the personality of nature was worshipped by them but they never attributed *tanüla* to the plants and animals. Come to think of it their religion cannot be termed as animism.

4. She fell in love with the tree

They did not have a negative frightening impression of nature. Nature for them cannot be termed as *mojing* (evil) because it was believed to be their protector and helper. However, after their conversion to Christianity it was labelled as evil.

Student: It is clear to us that the force of nature they worshipped cannot be termed as some vague spirit. The ancestors regarded nature as the protector and sustainer of their life.

Meyawati Walling: That is correct. Our activities and life, circled around the changing seasons. The *yangyang* bird will chirp and communicate to us the coming of the new *tsüngküm* (season). Plants and trees showed the season to us through their buds and fruits. In order to know the seasons accurately, we follow the position of the moon. Nature does not speak with us as we do with fellow human beings but the natural forces communicate to us and guide us about the changes of season in their own way. Even the wild flowers that bloom in the jungle have their sequence of blossoming according to the changing seasons. Thus human beings know how the seasons come and go.

Visitor: Do they attribute something like consciousness to nature?

All three of them: No.

Teacher: It was for a pragmatic reason. Men respected nature but did not have a common consciousness with it.

Visitor: What about the story of an Ao princess's marriage with a tree that stood tall by the riverside? There is the story of a woman falling in love with a tree and making a dao-belt for the tree. Now, someone with whom you have nothing in common other than being their protector, how would we explain the bond of love between them?

Student: On hearing of their affair, the villagers decided to cut down the tree. When the tree fell down on the ground, the tree reacted and showed a sign. So, the story signifies something about the tree having something like consciousness.

Teacher: There are stories describing how the tree sang a song for the young lady. There is also the belief that human beings learnt to sing from the tree.

Student: Yes there are also many stories about marriage that took place between man and animals. Our confusion is, if the trees and animals do not possess anything in common with man at all how come, marriage, relationship and communication took place between them? We want to be clear about this.

Tako Jamir: There is a story about a young couple. In olden days, young unmarried girls used to go and sleep in the *tzüki* (girl's dormitory). The owner of the dormitory should be a widow. If the widow is from Pongener clan, then all young girls from Pongener clan will go to her place to sleep for the night. So, young men from Jamir and Longkumer clan can visit the young girls at night. If the widow is from Jamir clan, then all the young girls from Jamir clan will go to her *tzüki* to sleep for the night. So, young men from Pongener and Longkumer clan can visit the girls in their dormitory at night. This was unanimously decided in the *arsalang* (cane platform) at Chungliyimti (the first Ao settlement). Through this practice, marriage within the same clan was avoided and it became a taboo. This is a story of that time: One night, a young handsome man came to the *tzüki* (girl's dormitory) but nobody knew his whereabouts. A young girl from the dormitory fell in love with him. During the festival of *moatsü* (the biggest and most important festival of the Aos) this girl gifted him a *nokleptsü*. *Nokleptsü* is a belt men wear around their waist. She was looking forward to watching him dance during the festival with his new belt on, but he did not turn up. She wondered what had happened to him. The next day, early in the morning, she went to fetch water from the stream and to her surprise she saw the same belt which was gifted to her boyfriend wrapped around the stem of a tree by the side of the river. She concluded that perhaps she had fallen in love with a tree who transformed itself into a young handsome man. There are exceptions like this story. However, our forefathers never thought that such things are common.

Imtinochet Jamir: As I said earlier, to understand our forefathers we must listen to the songs which have come down to us through endless generations. One song is about a woman named Matsüngchetla from the Pongen clan. One morning, she went to fetch water from the stream. After she washed and cleaned her face and feet, she thought of singing a song. So, she began to sing *tsüsenjoker, tsüsenjoker* (let me be refreshed, let me be refreshed). The next day, she went to fetch water again and began to sing the same song but after the two words she could not think of any more and she returned home. One the third day, an *aremsüng* tree responded to her song.

Tetzür: "Tsüsenjoker, Tsüsenjoker",
Süngdong: Chungliyimtilar Matsüngchetla ketang pongoa

English translation:

Woman: Let me be refreshed, let me bathe
Tree: The lady from Chungliyimti Matsüngchetla's hands arc bcautiful.

So it is from the tree that human beings learnt how to sing.

P. Ato. Jamir: There are stories of this kind, but we never know whether it was really the tree that helped her complete the song. Perhaps, she got inspiration from the rustling of the leaves of the tree and thought that the tree spoke to her. It is more of a special connection between her and the tree.

Visitor: It is only if we allow the possibility of communication between them that we can understand the likelihood of a union, such as love between them. This has larger implications. If trees are to be viewed as just dead matter, then they are only good enough to be used by humans. Why did the ancient elders prohibit the exploitation of nature?

Teacher: Man has *tanüla* and animals do not but this does not imply that they should not respect them. But in the modern world-view there is no *tanüla* at all, the concept is not there. In the Ao world-view man has *tanüla* and animals do not, that is an important aspect of the Ao world-view. They value differences. The moment you accept this, it is not difficult to understand this.

Visitor: Although there is no intermediate substance in common the tradition seems to highlight their feelings of togetherness with animals and nature.

The Nature of Nature

Teacher: The concept of solidarity in the midst of differences is very much a part of their understanding. If we cannot accept and locate ourselves in this understanding, than we won't be able to understand them. The idea of solidarity in the midst of differences is I think very much the core of their philosophy.

Visitor: Could we think of another term in place of consciousness, a neutral term such as "force"? If so, is it seen as a good or a bad force?

Teacher: They use the word *yimya*, signifying nature's way. Something like the nature of nature, the nature of river, the nature of mountain and so on. This I think is a very common notion in the Ao world-view. It can mean character, personality, etc. So, there is both bad and good *yimya* or, if you like, force. At times, they are scared of them and at other times, they respect them because nature protects them in times of trouble. Why we find it very difficult to understand is because we are so blinded by the dichotomy of man and nature. In the literal sense, they were sacred and they revered them. They were afraid of the nature of nature. They were scared because they did not understand the meaning of *yimya* or nature's way. In that sense, there is a consciousness. Of course, again that may not be the right word.

Student: The word consciousness does not capture the literal meaning of *yimya*. Is there a corresponding word in Ao vocabulary for *yimya*?

Imtinochet Jamir: In Ao vocabulary, we do not have a corresponding term for *yimya*.

Arsashi Jamir: As far as my understanding goes, everything on earth was created by a creator god. So, in return for nature's blessings and protection humans respected nature.

Merazulu Longchar: According to my understanding making concrete buildings and saving crores of rupees in the bank will not make a land rich. A rich land is known by its flora and fauna. In earlier times, elephants used to pass through Mokokchung town, tigers were found everywhere in the land, hornbills birds and bears were seen everywhere. We have seen large pythons in the forest but now these have disappeared because we hunted them down. Elephants and tigers won't be able to survive in open space today; times are so bad for them.

Student: Did they believe that all animals, plants and nature have equal powers which made them worship them all?

All of them: Yes.

Temsula Ao: Amongst all of them, if we have to make a hierarchy, animals will be at the lower rung. Human beings and nature including the plants, air, water, mountains, and land will be at the higher rung. We can also understand from the use of animals while performing the rituals that animals are in the lower rung.

Merazulu Longchar. If somebody falls sick, the fortune teller will tell you "it is because that tree or that mountain is unhappy, that this person is sick". Then somebody has to be identified who is going to speak to God, and who is going to perform the sacrifice. Once he is identified he has to go through a purification rite. He cannot accept tea or anything even from his own children. Then he has to be anointed so that he can become the interceder.

If there has to be a hierarchy then animal will be the lowest and nature would be at the highest and then comes man. Nature is crucial.

Guru Sademmeren Longkumer: Incidentally let me tell you something interesting. The stories of the girl falling in love with the tree and also with the river, marks the beginning of music amongst the Aos. Till that time, the Aos did not have any songs but from then on the practice of singing and song composing began. This may be taken as another indication of the Ao belief that nature can add great value to human life.

Visitor: So, we reach the important conclusion that nature is not unconscious.

XI

Evil

Visitor: Let us now move on to *temenen* (evil force). Can it be referred to as the devil or the Satan?

Tako Jamir: In olden days, *temenen* was thought to be an evil force that lives in marshy lands, lakes, rivers, big trees and rocks. We cannot see *temenen* with our naked eyes but from time to time man encounters *temenen*. When we roam alone in deep jungle, a person at some distance can see the movement of the *temenen* near another person but the person who is near *temenen* won't be able to see it. At times, we see them and at other times, we do not see them. At the time when Ao ancestors lived in Chungliyimti, they used to wander who was the *tambu* amongst the creatures: man, evil forces (*temenen*) or animals, for our ancestors had seen *menen mojing* (evil) holding a torch and going into the deep jungle. They worshipped *temenen* out of fear and offered it smoked meat which they kept at home.

Nungshimangyang Longchar: In olden days, any sickness or disease was believed to be caused by *mojing* (evil force). So, in order to ward off the evil force in man they took the help of *arasentsür* (soothsayer) who can see in her trance what was the cause of the person's sickness. The instruments used for divining sickness were somewhat different for men and women. For a male person she used a *lingra* (bamboo rope); by splitting the *lingra* she could find out in which place and by what force he caught the affliction. If the sick person was a female she used *amwa* (banana leaf) and followed the same procedure.

Once they knew the real cause of the sickness they performed rites to *tsüngrem* (god). All the village elders and relatives who are willing, will go and assemble in the sick person's courtyard. Here they will decide with a method called *melendangba* who will be sent to complete the ritual. Among the selected persons, one of them has to perform the rites by holding the *anvong* (cock basket) and rest of them carry the pig and the cock. The person who has to perform the rites in the fields goes near the sick person, fans him and tells the *mojing* to release him before they proceed to the fields. If the *mojing* caught him in the field they make a feast and perform rites by sacrificing animals to the field god. If it is in a far-off place and in deep jungle, they perform the ritual on the roadside. Incidentally, if the sick person is diagnosed with an incurable disease, he/she is shifted to *asangki/achangki*. In olden days *asangki* refers to a thatched house, built using a variety of fern leaves by the villagers at the outskirt of the village so that the afflicted person can live there away from fellow villagers.

Arsashi Jamir: *Temenen* cannot be seen; we can feel their movements but cannot see them with our naked eyes. As it has been reported by those who have come across these forces, we feel their presence around us, hear different sounds but we cannot see them. When they are around, the pigs make noises. In order to drive *temenen* away we pick up pebbles and throw at the place where we think it is, and spit in that direction.

Merazulu Longchar: Please remember, human beings were never scared of any animals, they were only scared of *temenen*. *Temenen* was forever looking for opportunities to harm human beings when they had to sleep in the *mesüjemlu* (field). To outwit him, they would cut a banana tree and put on their makeshift bed in the field. As they returned home they could see *temenen*, from a distance chopping the banana trees mistaking them to be human beings. Tigers, bears and snakes killed only those people who were fated to be killed by them.

Teacher: *Temenen*, it appears, is not an equivalent of the devil, for in *Temenen*'s case, men can negotiate with it in order to drive it away. *Temenen* actually is not the Christian devil. It is not a sin that I commit if I negotiate with *temenen*.

Student: I was told by my father that he had personally encountered *temenen*. It has a form which cannot be felt by

5. Aonglemla

our touch; it can appear and disappear in a flash of a second. When *temenen* moves around, the things on its path will shake. If there is pigsty around, the pigs will make noise and even the branches of trees will sway, that is how they felt the presence of the *temenen* (evil force). If such things happen then it was an indication that something bad will befall the villagers.

Tako Jamir: Suppose, three of us went to the jungle, only one person can feel the *temenen*. It is not necessary that all three of us can feel and see it. Even if I tell the others, they may not feel and see it.

Teacher: These forces we must remember are not actively evil. The actively evil ones are *mojing*s (ghosts).

Tako Jamir: There are many stories about how the ghost took man away from the village to different locations. In the year 1985, I had personally experienced this. One day past mid-night, I went to my village from the town. There is a forest between the town and the village. As I walked on the main road, I saw in front of me something like a black shawl on the other side of the road. I thought somebody must have dropped the shawl. It was 1 o'clock in the morning. On a close look at the black object, I realized that it was an *aonglemlatsü*, the creature who points her feet backwards and has long thick hair almost touching the ground. She started walking slowly but I was almost running in order to chase the creature away. Her laughter could be heard from far-off places. I finally reached home but I could still hear her laughter. A month passed; someone came to tell me that my brother suddenly died one month ahead of his 21st birthday. I went to my parent's home. On my way to my parent's home, I heard the same laughter that I had heard earlier from this creature. It then suddenly dawned on me that it had already warned me of the sudden death of my brother.

Let me tell you of another incident. This is about Purtoshi from Khensa village. Suddenly one day Purtoshi's father disappeared and nobody knew of his whereabouts. Just as suddenly, after a few days, he returned home. After this, Purtoshi noticed that whenever a *noktisüla* (a type of grasshopper) comes and makes sound inside the house, his father would behave in a strange way. He would make desperate attempts to run away and he had to be stopped forcibly. One day Purtoshi and his father were on their way to the church; suddenly the evil force attacked his father again and he ran into the backyard of a house and disappeared. Till today nobody knows whether he is still alive or dead. Every village has similar stories.

Teacher: One important thing to be noticed in all such cases is that if you get frightened or show your fear when you encounter such *temenen* then you will be carried away by it. So, one has to be fearless and challenge the *temenen* and overcome the evil force.

Tako Jamir: After the sudden death of my own brother I realized that the appearance of *temenen* was the foreboding of some impending disaster. It was an omen for my family as our ancestors had said. That is why as a precaution, if we meet *mojing* on our way home, we never go straight home. We either talk to some people thinking the presence of another person will stop the *mojing* from following us or spit on the pebbles and throw them away out into the open or urinate outside the house. It is believed that *mojing* is scared of our urine. So, before we enter the house, we should urinate outside the house facing the path along which we came. It is taken as overcoming the *mojing*. On reaching home sometimes we used to throw a burning log from the hearth into the the front courtyard of the house.

Visitor: Your description of *aonglemlatsü* reminds me of another evil force called *aonglemla*? Do they represent the same evil agency?

Student: Yes. Both these words are used to describe a creature which is supposed to occupy a place between man and God. She has long hair touching the ground and her feet point backwards.

Tako Jamir: *Aonglemla* is female lives in haunted places and in deep jungle. Sometimes she disguises herself in the form of a human being. She looks like a dwarf with long hair reaching to the ground and her feet points backwards though she has proper legs like humans. She can speak and laugh. Her laughter can be heard from a great distance and felt as if she is near. Meeting such a creature and hearing her laugh is a sign of bad tidings. This creature was not worshipped at all and was thought of as a spirit who lives in deep jungles. Apart from these, there are a host of other spirits who are associated with small streams, lakes, rivers, stagnant water, etc. which cause illness. Of these the fiercest one is the Mosaknü Tsüngrem (god who lives in lakes and marshland). Anyone caught by this *tsüngrem* never survives. Even to this day, people avoid lands with lakes and marshland for farming because of the fear of being caught by *tsüngrem*.

Guru Sademmeren Longkumer: *Aonglemla* is the name of a female creature that lives in deep jungle. In olden days, when people used to go for head-hunting, they were told that they would meet many *aonglemla*s in the plains of Akhumlenden where snakes and turtles were found in abundance. Therefore, when people used to go head-hunting in the plains of Akhumlenden, they would carry their load in a bag and the bags were placed upon several snakes and turtles on reaching the plains of Akhumlenden. As the snakes and turtles moved away, their bags would drop to the ground. At this point *aonglemla* would call out the names of the persons whose bags fell on the ground. Her voice would reassure the persons who felt lonely in the jungle. That is why it is said that we need not fear the jungle for she is the light of the jungle and that her laughter warms up the entire jungle so that we feel less deserted when we walk through it. If we don't harm her she won't do anything to us. She is the best amongst the *mojing*s, the least harmful of all the creatures that humans were afraid of.

Teacher: She is a character about whom most contradictory statements are made in the tradition.

Student: I have learnt from my grandfather that if *aonglemla* shouts at you while roaming in the jungles then it is considered a bad omen. Is this true?

Merazulu Longchar: That is not so. For her laughter, as we said just now, is good for the traveller; so how can she, then, be a bad omen? Meeting such creatures is both a blessing and also a sign that there might be an accident. Let me tell you a story. One day, my aunt went to her field and saw *aonglemla* lying naked in her farmhouse so she pushed her with her *serafu* (umbrella made of Latania leaves). You must note that she resembles human beings closely. My aunt told us that she does not have long hair but her body hair which is very long, makes it look so and her feet are pointed backwards. We can never see the satan but she can be seen. On being prodded with the umbrella she left my aunt's field, but on that very day, one of my aunt's children died.

Imtinochet Jamir: Unlike other extraordinary creatures, *aonglemla* is visible and can make her presence felt. People have actually seen this creature walk away with her feet pointed backward. But she is not entirely evil for she can do both evil and good.

Longdangsüja Mongru: Suppose we did not perform the proper ritual of propitiating nature or we opposed nature's way, the way we worship the stone god, for instance, then the *mojing* took revenge on us. There are only two options. Either your action will earn his wrath or get her blessings. Here one's own *tiya* will not save one from her wrath or make blessings effective. If we humbly perform the ritual properly nothing will happen. Thus pleasing *mojing* depends on one's actions. Both good and bad actions go along with one's *tiya*.

Teacher: What he is trying to say here is that your *tiya* itself will not save you.

Tako Jamir: There are other bad forces known as *semyasemko*. Suppose, I went to the jungle with my uncle and he senses and feels the bad forces in the jungle. Then, he will not say "some bad forces are around, it's better we go back home early". We never say on the spot that *temenen* is around but always in an indirect way. The person who feels it might say, "*mopungtamajung* (bad smell) is in the air".

Visitor: Can the *temenen* attack the non-Aos, the *Bendanger*, and the outsiders?

Tekatia Imchen: Yes. And all unnatural deaths, e.g. in child birth, due to drowning, falling down from trees or high cliffs, are attributed to *temenen*. In the case of actions which go against custom such as, boys and girls from the same clan getting married, and other wrong doings, the observance of certain rituals is prescribed to protect society from their evil effects. Violations of customary law, we must remember, are to be treated more seriously, because while unnatural events are beyond man's control, violations of social rules and regulations are not.

Visitor: Are such violations unforgiveable?

Temsula Ao: Not exactly. We can say this much; getting married within the same clan invites higher punishment.

Nungshimangyang Longchar: For this kind of marriage the entire village will mourn for a whole day and the verdict for the banishment of the couple from the village will be announced. The priest will carry a piglet whose testicles have not yet formed on a bamboo, and say that since these two have done this misdeed so they are being driven out of the village. This was one way of cleansing the village. It was considered the greatest sin and when a priest utters these words, it is like the verdict of the Supreme Court. There is no appeal beyond that.

Longrimongba Mongru: In the times of our ancestors, it was believed that all the sickness and diseases were caused by *mojing*.

In order to heal their sickness they took the help of *arasentsür* who could tell in her trance exactly the kind of sickness the patient is suffering from. *Arasentsür* used a method of splitting *amwa* (banana leaf) from which she could make out where and how the evil force had caught the victim.

Student: Can one conclude from all the discussion we have had so far that the Ao system of justice centred on the concept of truth and that for them truth is a universal law?

Pangchenmeren: Yes, truth is above all and is the highest of all.

Visitor: What is the Ao word for truth?

Pangchenmeren: The Ao word for truth is *ochi*.

Visitor: What about the moon and the sun? Are they truthful?

Saṭiba Jamir: Yes. Moon and sun are believed to be truthful because they are made by God. God is truth so is the moon and the sun; the moon and the sun give men the right time of day and night and divide the seasons.

Visitor: We can safely conclude that man, God and the natural forces, they all have to abide by the law of *ochi* or truth?

Guru Sademmeren Longkumer: Yes, they believed that God made the earth and he is truthful. Therefore, we eat the soil after committing mistakes. God asks the guilty why he came to such a state that he had to eat the soil and wait for God to punish him.

Merazulu Longchar: Let me clarify the point. Suppose I am a victim of some wrongdoing it is God who created me, who will take action against the wrongdoer and not me. We lived our life with that faith.

XII

Of God and Gods and their Work

Visitor: "God was believed to be the giver of man's destiny. Therefore, we were told to be truthful in all our conduct." This is the general view about the foundation of morality. Also the elders emphasized the centrality of truth and its equation with God and they have urged that we reflect with greater concern on the Ao notion of God. So dear elders please tell me a little more about the Gods of the Aos.

Ariyongdang Longchar: Our ancestors believed in different gods. Alumong Tsüngrem (field god), Ayim Tsüngrem (village god), Tekong Tsüngrem (mountain god) and Demen Tsüngrem (god of roads), were some of the important ones.

Sashimeren Walling: There is countless number of inferior and superior gods believed and worshipped by the Ao ancestors. Some god was worshipped with eggs, others with cock and the fiercest gods were worshipped with *azü* (dog), *auk* (pig) and *masü* (cow). *Azü* and *auk* were offered in haunted places.

Longdangsüja Mongru: But when our ancestors invoked these gods individually, they were not conceived as limited by the power of other gods; they were regarded neither as superior nor inferior in rank. Each god to the mind of the devotee is as good as any other god.

Meyawati Walling: We have never spoken of the difference between the greater and smaller gods. All that we worshipped whether, the stones, trees, field and kini, we worshipped in the name of God. We mention *tsüngrem* (God) in all our rituals and sacrifices. We invoke blessings from the Teyanglur and Sobatiyaba Tsüngrem as well as Lijaba the creator of the earth.

Sashimeren Walling: The triumvirate of Anüngtsüngba Tsüngrem (god of the sky), Meyutsungba Tsüngrem (god of judgement) and Lijaba Tsüngrem (creator god) were generally regarded as the most powerful gods.

Teacher: These three gods: Lijaba, whose place is on earth; Anüngtsüngba, whose place is in the sky; and Meyutsungba whose place is in the land of the dead, along with other deities, receive many appellations in consequence of their greatness and diversity of functions.

Student: Let us start with a description of Lijaba, who is also known as the creator god.

Ariyongdang Longchar: According to a myth, when Lijaba began to create the world he took care to see that its shape and contours looked good with hills and plains properly proportioned stretching down to the plains of Assam. While Lijaba was in the process of making the Ao territory a cockroach called *Lepluarsangla* reported the arrival of the headhunters. So, in his hurry to escape from his enemy, Lijaba said "let it be as it is" and ran away.

Guru Sademmeren Longkumer: This is correct. Lijaba began to create the world in a proper way with few plains and valleys till the plains of Assam. Suddenly, *Tsüleplu* (a cockroach) informed him of the arrival of his enemies. So, in his hurry to escape from his enemies he made the topography of Aos in an extremely haphazard manner.

Meyawati Walling: All the creatures in the world are made by the gods. The owner of all his creations is *nisungsangla*. There is, however, no mention of which god made what part of creation. Our ancestors believed that Lijaba, which is another word for the Almighty God, created the world. The most important thing of his creation is that, while he was making the world, he said: *longrangkümang, yendenkümang* (let there be hills and plains). He made the land of Assam plain and made our land hilly. This is how our ancestors explained to us about the creation of Ao territory.

Tekatia Imchen: The place where Lijaba began his work is in

Tsümalima, an area in the plains of Assam that can be seen from Longkhum village. If Lijaba was displeased with human beings it was believed, there would be diseases in the land, and the harvest would be poor. Lijaba was displeased if people were untruthful and if they did not observe *genna*. In order to worship Lijaba Tsüngrem, thirty days of *genna* was observed by the chief and seven days by his followers before and after the rituals and sacrifices. Lijaba was regarded as the eldest god.

Rongsenwati Longchar: It is also said that Lijaba was the son of Tezoloumi. After a dispute with his two brothers, tiger and man, he went into the deep forest near a body of *tsütayongpang* (stagnant water) and disappeared into a grove of banana plants (*amtsarong*) angry because he did not get his share of the property. While leaving, he showed human beings how to make *entsükang* (egg basket) and told them to worship him.

Visitor: I would like the elders to throw light on this query of mine; does Lijaba have a form, a personality and what is his status and relationship with the other gods?

Korakaba Jamir: Lijaba Tsüngrem is the greatest god because he created the earth. Lijaba was worshipped once a year in a ceremony known as Lijabamong. He was worshipped with great respect and honour by every household, in order to invoke his blessings. Every household used to put away *porep* (an old clay pot) in front of their house to be picked up by Lijaba when he would visit them. If they did not do so, so it was believed, Lijaba would punish the family.

Temsula Ao: Please allow me to explain. As he said, Lijaba's status is the highest amongst the gods. The festival that is dedicated to him with strict formalities is to be observed by all the people. Each household would stick a leaf on the front doorpost and at night Lijaba would come and find out which household is observing or not observing the festival. Any house without a leaf means they are not observing him with the required formalities and something bad will befall them.

They are so scared that if there had been any shortcoming in the main worship, they do another worship to beg forgiveness from him so that no havoc came on them.

Visitor: Are there any more accounts of personal contact of Lijaba with humans?

Longrimongba Mongru: Man maintained harmony with God through offerings and sacrifice. Eggs, cocks, pigs and *amwa* were used in rituals and sacrifices. Everything was offered to their gods both, in order to invoke his blessings and also for the fear of havoc upon their life and family. If they knew God was displeased by their offerings they worshipped him for the second time by taking the help of *sangmore* (soothsayer) who would tell them what kind of an offering should be given to their God. Other than this, I do not know of any personal contact that humans had with him.

Merazulu Longchar: Let me tell you this story about Lijaba and his two daughters. One day, a person name Changkichalangba chased a boar but the boar escaped and went inside a hole. He followed the animal into the hole. Inside the hole he saw a young girl called Noktitela, and her sister husking rice. The girls started to talk to the man. On hearing a man entering his place, Lijaba came out and asked who he was. "I am Changkichalangba, sir. And I have come to ask for your daughter's hand in marriage." Noktitela was mature enough to get married so Lijaba let him marry her. After they got married, Lijaba gave them a pig and told the couple to work hard and cultivate the land along with all the villagers.

Well Changkichalangba did the opposite. He would go to every household and split a portion of their bamboo wall saying that since he had to repair their wall, he would have to stay in the house. While the rest of the villagers went to work in the field, he took a pig to a remote corner of the village, killed the pig and cooked it in a pot. On his way to meet him, Lijaba saw the pot of meat already cooked. He knew that since Changkichalangba wanted to eat all the meat alone he had not informed any of the villagers. So, Lijaba got angry and collected some *oksüjang* (a variety of nut with thorny shell) and put them inside the meat pot. Changkichalangba ate the meat, the thorny shell made him cry out in pain and he quickly spat out the thorny shell from his mouth, the thorns got stuck in the leaves of a tree. Till today, we can see that tree with holes in its leaves.

Then again, when our people were still living in Chungliyimti, it is said, Lijaba invited them all for a meal. He fed them with pork intestines and frogs. A man named Fongyangtsüng refused to eat the frog so Lijaba dug out a fish from the earth with his stick and served him the fish. While leaving Lijaba's place, Fongyangtsüng also did the same for Lijaba. These stories prove that our people believed that Lijaba lived among human beings.

Guru Sademmeren Longkumer: Lijaba Tsüngrem is believed to be the god of blessings. Let me also tell you a story about him. Once upon a time, there were two sisters who lived with their step-mother. One day, they decided to leave their home because they were ill-treated by their step-mother. They wandered through forests and fields until finally they came to a makeshift camp built by small children near the village. The elder sister asked the small children to lend their camp to them. Some of them were reluctant to give away their camp, but they agreed when she and her sister gave them some *monguzenojang* (a variety of fig) in exchange for the camp. This story is about these two orphans whom Lijaba helped to become rich. One day Lijaba came to this village where the two orphans lived. Their names were Akümbong and Yarla. He disguised himself in the form of an old man wearing rag clothes and looking filthy. He asked for shelter but nobody let him stay in their house as they were "observing *genna*". He was turned away with these words: "Our pigs have given birth to piglets, our hens have hatched chicks at home and we are observing *kimem* (to keep physically clean); so sorry we cannot make you welcome!" Finally, Lijaba came to a thatched house on the outskirts of the village where the two sisters were living. They were poor orphans, and yet they welcomed him to their home. When they told Lijaba they had no rice to cook, Lijaba began to scratch his knee murmuring something, and then a grain of rice appeared on his palm! When he put the grain of rice in the boiling water the single grain of rice became a potful, which was more than enough for the three of them! He told them to place the meat pot near the fire but they said they had no meat to cook. Lijaba began to scratch his knee and a slice of meat appeared on his palm which also turned into a potful of meat! The next morning he asked where their field was, they were too shy initially, to show him their tiny patch of rice field. When they finally showed Lijaba where their field was, Lijaba blessed their field and told them to harvest till their granary was full for as long as they lived; and he sang this song:

Akümbong o tenuna Lu,
Mo jungjangna,
Ayi tesaktsüla (Repeat twice)

English translation:

Let Akümbong and his sister's field,
Have healthy saplings,
Let there be no weeds in the field

Student: We have heard similar stories from our elders from other villages.

Longdangsüja Mongru: Originally the gods were all supposed to be equal in power but there was talk of some of them being superior to others. Let me sing for you a song that claims that Lijaba (the creator of the earth) is the greatest god:

Oh! kangkoteptai,
Lata kha alimana oh kangkoteptai,
Lata dangko semani zoni towaba,
Zoni dangko semani, changchanglong towaba;
Changchanglong dangko semani kevolong towaba,

Kevolong dangko semani,tsüsemlong towaba;
Tsüsemlong dangko semani,
Ora ningjangko;
Lijaba ali yangruba towabaota

English translation:

Oh! they are quarrelling,
The moon and the world are quarrelling,
I asked the moon God who is the greatest God?
He replied the sun God is the greatest God;
When I asked the sun God who is the greatest God?
He replied, Changchanglong God is the greatest God,
When I asked the Changchanglong God;
He replied Kevolong is the greatest God,
When I asked of the Kevolong God,
He replied Tsüsemlong God is the greatest God;
When I asked of the Tsüsemlong God,
He replied there in the foot hill of the earth,
Lijaba the creator of the earth is the Greatest God.

Tekatia Imchen: After Lijaba created the world he made trees and plants and made them grow. Then he made the animals including human beings. It is said Lijaba gave different colours to all the animals. Tiger, cheetah, deer, a bison and bear, each got a different look and the maker also gave a long tail to the rat. He finished giving different prints and looks to all the animals but the *yimpangmejongben* bird (magpie) arrived late as she was looking after her grandfather. So even though she was late, he gave her multiple colours on her beak, feet and feathers.

Longdangsüja Mongru: Whether Lijaba is the creator of animals and plants I do not know but I have heard that all the animals and plants belong to Lijaba. While Lijaba was in the process of making the Ao territory a cockroach called *Lepluarsangla* informed him of the arrival of the head-hunters. Therefore, out of shock he made the Ao territory in haste with its uneven and convoluted surface. This you have already heard from others.

Visitor: Thank you for telling us about the earliest speculations of the Aos about creation. Can we conclude from the discussion so far that gods were spoken of as possessing human forms and acting as human beings?

All of them: Yes.

Visitor: Are there any temples or churches that belong to Lijaba?

Elders: No.

Student: There are no temples or churches that belong to Lijaba but in Longkhum village there is a tiny patch of land which was believed to be Lijabali (Lijaba's land) so, in olden days, people used to go and worship Lijaba there.

Meyawati Walling: A word about the Lijabamong festival will be useful here. In this festival Lijaba was worshipped with the belief that it was he who created the earth. The village *patir* (priest) along with all the villagers will go to the outskirts of the village and pray for the well-being of the earth. After this is done, they will observe *amouer*: the villagers would stay indoors in their homes. The village main gate would be shut. All inhabitants would stay indoors and observe Lijabamong, the ritual connected with this festival.

Guru Sademmeren Longkumer: Here is a song sung during Lijabamong:

O! amongerani,
Longtitsüngba adokdangbo,
Sürem tajung apener,
Shiten chiyonga mongtini.

English translation:

O! we are celebrating,
The day Longtitsüngba comes to the village,
We put on new Sürem shawl,
And celebrate eating meat on this day.

Temsula Ao: Lijabamong was strictly observed with all the procedures because of the fear of causing havoc upon the people. All manual work was prohibited even by the slaves and stamping on the ground was not allowed. On the last day of the Lijabamong, the village chief priest offered a pig to Lijaba as a sacrifice on the outskirts of the village. It was believed that Lijaba visited every household that night. If he does not see the sprig of a scented herb called *jangpetwa* on the front door post, Lijaba will enter that house and kill one of the family members, that is why due respect was given to Lijaba so that people won't incur his wrath.

Teacher: The stress on the ancestors respecting Lijaba purely out of fear of calamities appears to be influenced by the scientific study of the so-called primitive religions. Let us try to be as free of bias as possible.

Ariyongdang Longchar: Then there is also the Tsüngremmong festival in which Lijaba is worshipped which is observed in the first week of August every year. Tsüngremmong is observed for three days and it was introduced by the Longsa Sangpur clan who saw gods playing a tug-of-war.

Here is a story about the festival of *aratsütep* (tug-of-war) as it is popularly called. One day, a man from Sangpur clan of Longsa village went to the jungle to collect *azü* (bamboo shoots) near the Tsülayong River. While he was walking along the river, he heard a loud noise on the other side of the river. As he peeped through the bushes, he saw both the male and female gods dancing and singing and also playing a tug-of-war in their full attire. They were singing the following song:

O! atsütepdini,
Par nongpur ar atsütepdini;
Oh! tsüla yongpanglar,
Süngzü atsütepdini.

English translation:

O! lets play tug-of-war,

The gods are playing with sword bean creeper;
Oh! the female gods on the bank of the Tsüla River.
Pull the rope.

Meyawati Walling: When our ancestors were still living in Chungliyimti, the Longsa Sangpur saw the gods enjoying a game of tug-of-war nearby. They liked the sight of the gods playing and began to imitate the gods and thus started the festival of *among*. The Longsa Sangpur was blessed by the gods and they became rich. Later, the practice spread in all the Ao territory and people started to observe the Tsüngremmong regularly.

Meyutsungba, The Supreme Judge

Student: Can we now proceed to the second deity of the triumvirate: Meyutsungba Tsüngrem (god of judgement)?

Tekatia Imchen: Meyutsungba is believed to be the god of justice. It is he who judges the souls when they reach his gate to enter the *asüyim* (land of the dead). As you have already heard, when a person dies his soul has to undergo a test in Meyutsungba's portal. It is said there is a *süngtidong* (big tree) standing in his courtyard. Every soul has to pierce the tree, men used *nü* (spear) and women used *anüm* (an instrument used in weaving by womenfolk). Those who were successful were proved to be the truthful ones and those who failed were proved to be the untruthful ones. Truthfulness and honesty are emphasized so much in Ao society.

Kikasangla Imchen: We believe that the truthful ones will go to Motsüngba's portal. The truthful ones will go straight to Motsüngba's portal and the untruthful and thieves will go to his backyard.

Teacher: Mrs Kikasangla Imchen interestingly is using the word Motsüngba in the traditional way. While some of us are speaking of the god of justice as Meyutsungba which is the more modern usage.

Rongsenwati Longchar: Meyutsungba was known also as Molutsüngba, I agree with Mr Lipoknokdang who wrote a few pages about Molutsüngba in the year 1935-36. The meaning of Molutsüngba is "the god who sits in the ocean". Molutsüngba literally means "owner of the sea".

Satiba Jamir: It is said that objects which a person had stolen in his lifetime were taken along in a basket as he went down to Meyutsungba's portal. On the way, he tries to hide all the things in the bottom of his basket but when he reaches Meyutsungba's portal everything is seen as lying on top of his basket.

Rongsenwati Longchar: Our ancestors said the day a person dies he takes all the trophies of heads and animal skulls that he earned in his lifetime to Molutsüngba.

Nungshimangyang Longchar: A person who was unclean was not accepted by Molutsüngba in the land of the dead. *Nütsüdong* is a tree standing in Meyutsungba's courtyard. The thought of final judgement of the soul makes man to live an honest and righteous life on earth.

Visitor: This has been beautifully explained by the elders earlier. But please continue.

Nungshimangyang Longchar: There is a story that talks about the final judgement in Meyutsungba's portal. Once upon a time there lived a man called Nokshiluba in Longmisa village in Changchang colony. When he was still a bachelor he wanted to marry a lady named Menangsangla who was from the same village. But she refused his proposal so he was badly hurt and made up his mind to take revenge on her. After a while he got married to another lady. Meanwhile, Menangsangla also became old and was doing *arasentsür mapa* (work of a soothsayer). Though he was married to another woman, Nokshiluba could not forget what had happened between them in the past always looking for a chance to take revenge on her.

One day, when Menangsangla was away from her home,

Nokshiluba purposely took a new *pakti* (mat) from his house and kept it in her porch, to accuse her of stealing the mat. Before she returned home Nokshiluba informed the villagers that his new mat was missing from his house. So, he along with *tsütenmonger* (village guard) went to each and every household in search of it. At last, they found it in Menangsangla's porch. When he informed the village council about the incident they decided to fine her an *auk* (pig). Menangsangla pleaded innocence but the village council ruled her out.

Menangsangla offered the village council: to lift a tiger's head, or to chop cock's nape or to hoist grains of rice, to know the truth. These were the three methods of judgement practised in olden days. But the village council was not convinced.

Teacher: Let me explain the three possible ways of determining the innocence of an accused in a case of misconduct:

(i) *Keyi kolak ajongba* (lifting the skull of a tiger): In order to prove that you are in the right you lift the skull of a tiger and say these words: "If I have done anything wrong against my friend turn me into a tiger's skull".

(ii) *An kong alangba* (chopping the nape of a cock at one go): The accused says these words as after he holds the cock by its wings: "my friend accused me of doing wrong but I have not done any wrong. God of justice acquit me as I chop the cock's nape".

(iii) *Jangkang asong* (hoist the grain of rice basket): Three grains of rice are packed tightly in clean banana leaves and put in a small basket and following words are said: "O Sobatiyaba (god of destiny), *Ita-anü Tsüngrem* (moon-sun god) I have done nothing wrong but my friend accuses me of doing wrong today, god of justice acquit me". Both of them together hang the grain basket in the fork of a tree. If the grains of rice are found separated from each other and if there is dust in between the grains, then the person accused was guilty.

This took place in a place called Ngayatang in the company of the village *putir* (priest) and elders. They returned home after it was over led by the person who won the case followed by his opponent and village *putir* and the elders.

Nungshimangyang Longchar: The day the village council fined her an *auk* (a pig), Menangsangla declared to the whole village that she will die along with Nokshiluba. There in Meyutsungba's portal the god of justice will decide the case and establish the truth. She sang this song when she was accused of robbery by the village council and Nokshiluba:

Lata ayimyabanglana,
Zoni tsükrakola,
Nai ratetjangni, nai aijangni;
Keyi kolak ajongtsütitasüdi majungtsütida,
An kong alangtsüditasüdi malangtsülita;
Jangkang songtitasüdi müsongtsüdita,
Changchang longmisa yimbatirna,
Ni menangsangla oda wangshiryarma.

English translation:

Moon god who shines on the land,
Sun god if you rise up,
You enlighten, pronounce the judgement;
I want to lift the tiger's head but I was refused,
I want to chop the cock's nape but I was refused;
I want to hoist the grain basket but I was refused;
Longmisa Changchang village council,
Why are you troubling Menangsangla like this?

When she learnt of Nokshiluba's death, she, with her magical powers, put herself and her grandchild to death. She took her grandchild with her as witness to Meyutsungba's portal. In Meyutsungba's portal Nokshiluba failed to pierce the *süngtidong* with his spear, and it is said that all the souls of the dead who were in Diphu laughed at him. When she took her turn and pierced the tree with a loud noise the *diphusanger* (souls that live in the land of the dead) were jubilant over her victory. Suddenly, her grandchild came back to life and she told the villagers what had happened to Menangsangla and Nokshiluba. This story is an illustration of judgement in Meyutsungba's portal.

Satiba Jamir: Meyutsungba judges the soul. Truthful ones are allowed to live with him and the untruthful ones condemned to a miserable life. Unmarried women are allowed to roam in thick prickly bushes. It is customary to divide the household belongings of the dead person a couple of months after his death or with the change of season. If a person dies a few days before the Moatsü and Tsüngremmong festivals then they divide the household belongings after that.

Just as the Ao ancestors believed that there is life after death they also believed that the immortal soul is guided by *tiyar*. Therefore, we were told by our ancestors to be truthful to each other and to share our happiness with fellow human beings. Man must always remember that when a man dies, his soul has to undergo a test in the portal of Meyutsungba. It is he who judges the soul when they reach his gate to enter the land of the dead.

Teacher: It is not easy to give a consistent account of the varied speculations that have been going on about the gods. But we request you to satisfy the craving of our minds and tell us about the last of the triumvirate.

Ariyongdang Longchar: As has been said earlier, human beings believed and worshipped three different gods. Anüngtsüngba was the eldest one, next was Alitsüngba and the third one was Motsüngba. They invoke blessings from these three different gods by saying these words: "*Ah . . . ha aningka alina, lata kha, tsüngi kha, alitsüngba, motsüngba* we ask your blessings".

Visitor: Please now give us a description of the third God mentioned in the beginning: i.e. Anüngtsüngba.

Ariyongdang Longchar: Anüngtsüngba is the god of the sky. He is also referred to moon-sun god who has the power over the heavenly bodies and all the elemental forces like the rain, thunders and storms.

Nungshimangyang Longchar: In all the rituals and sacrifices they mention Anüngtsüngba, moon-sun god. When there is drought in the land men worship the wells and the lakes asking Anüngtsüngba to send down the rain to the earth singing this kind of song.

Alimako alir,
Oh! Anüngtsüngba,Kodaktsüngba,
Ali yangerbai tsünglu atir;
Oh! tsülapangko oh pakopangko,
Nena osü ajemer,
Alimako alir bilemtetangmano;
Oh! tinu yimsanger dang,
Chelo akatener tsümetsü shilangjangmano.

English translation:

People of the world,
Oh! God of the sky, the god above,
And the creators of the earth send down the rain;
Oh! on the bank of the river Tsüla and pako,
You both have mutual understanding,
And remember the people living on earth;
Oh! to your friends in the land,
Send them back the rain for the crops.

Student: Who was the most prominent god of the Aos?

Satiba Jamir: Anüngaliyanglusang *Tiyar* Tsüngrem.

Ariyongdang Longchar: It is said Anüngtsüngba (god of the sky) and Lijaba Tsüngrem (god who created the earth) were equally powerful but they fought with each other because both of them wanted to become the most powerful one. Anüngtsüngba was successful in subordinating Lijaba and he sent Lijaba down to the earth. Lijaba or Alitsüngba as he is also called, finally formally submitted to Anüngtsüngba and told him even if he had lost to him he'll remain the most powerful on earth and told Anüngtsüngba to be the most powerful god in the sky.

Tareptsüba: When Lijaba finally submitted to Anüngtsüngba, Lijaba decided that even though the loser, he would remain the most powerful god on earth while Anüngtsüngba himself, would be the most powerful one in the sky.

Visitor: Such differences of opinion are common when you are engaged in the task of describing the ancient deities. Please continue.

Merazulu Longchar: Of course Lijaba made the earth so he is great. But according to me god of sky is the highest for he made both the earth and the sky. Anyway, if Lijaba was the greatest god, he would have never come, met and lived with human beings. This is the way we now conceive of god.

Satiba Jamir: By the way I have also heard of the two deities in the realm of the sky god namely Atanghang and Metanghang. Whenever there were thunders it was believed that Atanghang and Metanghang were quarrelling in the sky.

Arsashi Jamir: Worship and prayers must begin by addressing the god of sky, and moon-sun god, giving thanks for their blessings and asking for forgiveness and long life. In order to determine the right or wrong of one's actions; the worshipper tries to pierce the stone either three times or six times depending on the decision of the village council. In front of the village chief priest and village elders, worshippers will lift up their spears and say these words to the stone god: "Oh god of the sky, moon-sun god, I have not done anything wrong against my friend but my friend accuses me of doing wrong. Today, the god of justice please acquit me". Both the accuser and the accused then try to pierce the stone with their spears one after another, after which they return home. They wait either for three days or for six days; if anything bad befalls on any one of them, his family or his party, he is proved to be in the wrong.

Longrimongba Mongru: Here is a song that speaks about the greatest god.

Anüng ali tsüngtako
Süba tezümbata semtsüdangani;
Nüngjang peti zoni dang nina semtsüdangani;
Ungerlongang tezümba oda,
Ungerlongdang nina semtzüdangani
Kheralongang tezümba oda,
Kheralongdang nina semtzüdangani kevolongdang toabaota,
kevolongdang nina semtzüdangani,
Anüng ali yanglusang jongpotemtem tezümbaota.

English translation:

Between the heaven and the earth,
I asked who the greatest god is.
I asked the sun and the star who the greatest god is
Ungerlong stone is the greatest god
I asked the Ungerlong god and he replied
Kheralong stone is the greatest god
I asked the Kheralong god and he replied
Kevolong god is the greatest god
I asked the Kevolong god and he replied
The god who made the earth and the sky Jongpotemtem is the greatest god.

Satiba Jamir: Jongpotemtem (another term for the god of sky), is the greatest god. It is said that the entire universe is leaning on Jongpotemtem's shoulders.

Student: How is Jongpotemtem the god of sky, the greatest?

Both of them: Lijaba is worshipped as a god who is the master of only the earth but Jongpotemtem, the god of the sky is regarded as the greatest god because moon and sun are also under him.

His greatness is described in the song above. We have not heard of any god greater than him.

Teacher: The term Jongpotemtem literally stands for chief, in this sense it can be referred to as the supreme or the chief god. He is said to hold the two powerful forces, the sky and the earth together. If not for the balance between the two that he provides, there would be fearsome consequences in the form of natural calamities.

Korakaba Jamir: While on the subject of gods let us not forget to include Awatsüng Tsüngrem (god of lakes) who was worshipped because he saved the villagers from their enemy. This god is said to rule over waters. There is a story about how Awatsüng Tsüngrem drove the Ao's enemies away. Once the warriors from Mopungchukit village went down to the plains of Assam and killed their king. So, the king's troops were sent to invade them. When the king's troops were about to destroy them, Awatsüng Tsüngrem stood in front of them. The soldiers were frightened to death and so they ran away. During harvest, they worshipped Awatsüng Tsüngrem and invited the different gods from other places in order to urge them for blessings for good harvest.

Student: Do Awatsüng Tsüngrem and the other gods signify one and the same reality?

Korakaba Jamir: Yes, they believed only in one god but worshipped this one god in different manners by giving different names. Lijaba, Meyutsungba and Anüngtsüngba are believed to be one god.

Kikasangla Imchen: Though we have different names for different gods, we believed that there is only one godhead.

Teacher: There is a lot of misunderstanding of the ancestors regarding this. Let Mr Bendangsashi Longchar explain the whole scenario to us.

Bendangsashi Longchar: In olden days, our ancestors lived together with gods. They observed different kinds of rituals and sacrifices in order to invoke divine blessings. If a child was born they observed *genna* for three days. *Ratsünlar* (soothsayer) was a mediator between *mojing* and human beings. They offered pigs and cocks to *mojing* after consulting a "soothsayer" in order to save themselves from all kinds of troubles and they observed Lijabamong (worship of Lijaba), Tsüngremamou (worship of gods) and Yimkülemmong (worship of the village) strictly so that god's wrath would not wreak havoc upon them. All the big stones were worshipped by our ancestors for their blessings. They performed all rituals correctly, otherwise they were punished by the stone god who caused them sufferings and pains.

Satiba Jamir: One interesting point which you must remember in connection with our gods is that in every village different gods were regarded as the fiercest ones. In my Mopungchukit village, Awatsüng Tsüngrem was regarded as the fiercest god, all lived in awe of him.

Longdangsüja Mongru: The friendly gods were Tesaraba, Tetiyaba, Tenokiba who guide and protect human beings. But Tesaraba was also regarded as *mojing* (evil).

Meyawati Walling: Allow me to clarify this. Our ancestors talk about Teyanglur Tsüngrem (creator god), Sobatiyaba (god of destiny), Tesaraba Tsüngrem and Tenokiba Tsüngrem. Sobatiyaba shapes our destiny on earth. Teyanglur made us, Tesaraba always wants to kill us and Tenokiba protects us from Tesaraba. Tesaraba threatens man with destruction while Tenokiba stops Tesaraba and protects people from his anger. Tenokiba saves us from Tesaraba by promising the latter that he will give him what he wants. Sobatiyaba is the one who gives us the *tiya* (fate). Tetiyaba as he is also called gives us our share of blessings and misfortunes in the world.

Student: It is said female gods are fiercer than the male gods?

Merazulu Longchar: Yes, female gods were fiercer than the male gods.

Yabangchila Imchen: There are both bad and good female and male gods. Yes, if we are caught by a female *mojing* (evil) then our illness will be prolonged. Whereas, if a male *mojing* caught us and we fall sick, we will recover from our illness quickly. There are fierce female *mojing*s. In pregnancy, if we are caught by a female *mojing* then the unborn child will die in the mother's womb. If we see a male god holding us then it was viewed as a precursor of good tidings.

Korakaba Jamir: I have not heard about the female and male gods in the Ao traditional belief system but when they talked about *mojing* (evil) and *arasentsür* (soothsayer) they distinguished between female and male *mojing*s but no female *tsüngrem* (god) is ever mentioned. Human beings believed that while *tsüngrem* gave blessings, *mojing* causes sufferings and pains and does all kinds of evil.

Bendangsashi Longchar: But all the while, our ancestors believed only in one god called Avo Lijaba. He was the god of both blessings and punishments. Human beings gave different names to all the natural things they considered big and anything that frightened them.

Longrimongba Mongru: In my understanding too, they believed only in one *tsüngrem* (god). However, with the advent of Christianity to the land the talk about the Ao belief in many gods started. But in olden days they believed only in one god. Lijaba Tsüngrem, Meyutsungba Tsüngrem, Anüng Tsüngrem, Along Tsüngrem were mentioned in rituals and sacrifices. Undoubtedly, in Longkhum village, the villagers even worshipped a host of *tenem*s (mountains) like Rituyimtok, Liangchen and Longlangba Long. Whenever they performed rites and rituals they used to mention the names of those gods. But we should not forget that they signify only one god.

XIII

Of Moon and Sun

Visitor: Just as you have talked about the mountain gods, can you also throw some light on the divinity of moon and sun?

Longdangsüja Mongru: Ao ancestors worshipped Ita-anü Tsüngrem (moon-sun god) because he gave light to them. If there was many deaths in their family and they were not blessed by material possessions, they thought perhaps Ita-anü Tsüngrem did not like them at all. They never thought of the evil deeds their great grandfathers, grandfathers and their fathers had done. Whenever there was lunar and solar eclipse nobody went to the fields and jungles but stayed at home feeling pity for the moon because they thought during eclipse the tiger was eating the moon.

Temsula Ao: I am of the opinion that moon-sun god is not there in the Ao pantheon, though we did have Anüngtsüngba, god of the sky.

Korakaba Jamir: No No. Ita-anü Tsüngrem (moon sun god) might not have been worshipped but he was definitely mentioned in all the rites and rituals. During different seasons, all the rituals and sacrifices were performed in order to invoke blessings from this god.

Longdangsüja Mongru: Ita-anü Tsüngrem was never worshipped but it was believed that if Ita-anü god is pleased and shines upon human beings they become rich; if he does not shine upon them they remain poor on earth. Here is a story about three brothers. In a family there were three brothers. The eldest two became very rich but the youngest one continued to remain poor no matter how much effort they made to help him out. So, they asked the Ita-anü Tsüngrem why he made their younger brother poor?

Ita-anü asked "Do you have a younger brother?" When they

said yes they were told to stand in line early in the morning along with their brother when the sun rises up. They did so. But when the sun rose up early in the morning he passed them without noticing their younger brother again. The younger brother remained poor as ever! Therefore, from that day onwards Ao ancestors believed that if Ita-anü Tsüngrem does not notice one's face those people always remain poor on earth.

Ariyongdang Longchar: Not only mountains, sun and moon but all big objects and natural things such as *süngdonglidong* (trees and plants), *long* (rocks), *tenemtem* (mountains) and *tsüta* (marshland) have force and can influence human events, therefore they were in awe of them.

Nungshimangyang Longchar: I can give you an account of a river-god. After the Mongsen-speaking people had a misunderstanding over some issues with the Chungli speakers, the Mongseners stopped going to worship the stone god. Instead they began to worship a river called Sartiyong. This is a song sung by the Sartiyong, the river god.

O! atong alina,
Asen atong alina;
Mongsen tsüba tsüngremi,
Nükümli memerakana.

English translation:

O! friends on earth,
Our friend on earth;
The River god of Mongsener
Doesn't approve of your habitat.

Sartiyong River was the only river god worshipped by the villagers after Süngratsü village was founded. There are different gods in the Ao belief system but it is said they believed only in one god.

Ariyongdang Longchar: In sacred places of worship even

6. The Guardians

spitting was not allowed and regarded as taboo. *Auk* (pig), *antepong* (cock) and *entsü* (eggs) are the three things used in rituals and sacrifices. If you are interested we can tell you how the different gods were worshipped:

(i) *Lumongtsüngrem (field god):* Field god was worshipped in the fields by hoisting six *aouterok* (six bamboo sticks) near the *alukima* (farmhouse). After the jungle was slashed and burnt, an egg and two cocks were taken to the field on different days to offer to Lumong Tsüngrem. While sowing, they took *auk* and *jangpetwa* (a scented herb). *Jangpetwa* was stuck on the front door of the farmhouse. Some *jangpetwa* was also kept inside the pots. Once this is done, they invoked his blessings by saying these words: "we have come to worship you with this *auk* and *jangpetwa* bless us with good health and good harvest". After they said these words, a few pieces of half-cooked meat, *avu* (beer) and *atsa* (rice) were offered and kept on an *amwa* (banana leaf) for the field god. All these rituals and sacrifices were performed regularly till the harvesting season.

(ii) *Kitzüngmong (worship of house): Kitzüngmong* was performed by the couple in order to sanctify their house. On that day no visitors were allowed to enter the house and all the doors in the house were kept shut. Even their own children were not allowed to be at home. Except the couple, no one including their own children was allowed to partake of the cooked food.

Korakaba Jamir: But please note that the rites performed for different gods differ in different places of worship.

(iii) Yimrong Külemba: Six feathers of the bird *antepong* are used in the worship of the sacred location of the village. Only the words used in addressing the deity may be different from place to place. Some use the following words. ;

O! yimkong tsüngrem,
Ita-anü tsüngrem,
Longmisa akümdang, makibaanpong,
Hatibakhuben oh ajita aruani,
kübo makibai külemer kübo hatibai külemer dang ozüi külemer.

English translation:

O! God of all
Moon-Sun God
When Longmisa village was formed Makiba carried the anpong
Hatiba carried the load
This is how we came
As my grandfathers Makiba and Hatiba worshipped you
Now we worship you.

When the village was being formed my grandfather came carrying the cock and the load. He would invoke the deity with these words, "As my grandfathers Makiba and Hatiba worshipped you in the past, I worship you now". Ansülong is a name of a stone god in Süngratsü village. It was formerly known as Ansükong. There are people who still worship this stone god.

Nungshimangyang Longchar: Yes, in our village it is said Ansülong Tsüngrem used to kill our pigs, if he was not satisfied with the pig that they offered him, they made it a point to search for a bigger one.

One God Monotheism/Polytheism

Guru Sademmeren Longkumer: Although, the tradition speaks of so many gods, the ancient Ao religion can be said to be monotheistic. They believed only in one god called, Teroktsünger who is the creator, preserver and moral governor of the universe. So great and powerful was Teroktsünger that people never mentioned his name when they worshipped him. They addressed him as moon-sun god, lord of the sky instead. Lord of the sky, moon-sun god are metaphorical expressions for Teroktsünger. Teroktsünger is also called Sobatiyaba because of the belief that human beings came to this world through him and it is he who determines their fate and destiny. It is said Teroktsünger is supreme among all the gods mentioned. Here is a song which says Teroktsünger is the greatest and the eldest among all the gods.

O menang ali poker,
Süba towabata,
Yimkangkoina pangjem;
Lata dangko yusemtsü, Zoni dangko yusemtsüina,
Süba towaba charoa;
Anüng ali yanglusang jongpongtemtem,
Teroktsünger towabaona;
Anüng ali yanglusüna,
Lijabatsü anungjakona,
Esung nisunger asü-aküm tetajen,
Meyutsungba pana kümona.

English translation:

When the earth was created,
Human beings asked,
Who is the supreme God?
He asked the moon-sun God,
Moon-sun God replied;
God who made the sky and earth,
Teroktsünger is the supreme;
Though, Lijaba is the creator of the earth,
He is lower than Teroktsünger;
God who divides life and death,
Meyutsungba was also made by Teroktsünger.

Rongsenwati Longchar: This is the correct picture. There is only one god but human beings gave different names to him like Longtitsüngba and Anüngtsüngba. These were merely different names for the same god according to his different domains like fields and homesteads. In rituals and sacrifices they mentioned Tekong Tsüngrem (mountain god), Yongpang Tsüngrem (river god) and Mosakni Tsüngrem (god of stagnant water) though they have never seen them at all. Mosakni Tsüngrem was believed to be the fiercest god. Purtongzük in his research paper has mentioned twenty-two gods but gods believed in by the Ao ancestors were countless.

Kikasangla Imchen: Yes, Ao ancestors believed in many gods but I won't be able to give the exact number to you. I have lost my memory and have forgotten many things.

Rongsenwati Longchar: Field god was worshipped in the field. If a person had stomach upset while working in the field or some other sickness he/she assumed that it was the work of Yongpang Tsüngrem.

The owner of the field offered a dog to the field god and cursed the place by saying these words "whoever comes to cultivate this land, he should offer a dog to you each time he cultivates this land".

Satiba Jamir: Tradition speaks of Lijaba Tsüngrem, Ita-anü Tsüngrem, Teyanglur Tsüngrem and *Tiyar* Tsüngrem. However, in times of illness they offered pigs and hens only to Awatsüng Tsüngrem (god of lakes) for they held this god to be responsible for sickness and disease.

Student: We can conclude with confidence that our ancestors believed in many many gods. These gods were invoked for offspring, victory in battle, destruction of enemies, and the preservation of the health and wealth of the worshippers.

Visitor: And also that each god has his own domain, and is equal in power to others. Are we correct?

Merazulu Longchar: All the gods have their own domain. All of them use their powers according to their own capacities and there are no conflicts of power amongst them.

Visitor: But we have been told about a fight between the water god and the fire god competing for power.

Meyawati Walling and Yabangchila Imchen: Both water and fire were regarded as most important by our ancestors because the water sweeps away everything without leaving anything and the fire burns up everything into ashes. We were told that no other elements can compete with them. There was a fight between fire and water and water is said to have won the fight.

Longrimongba Mongru: Yes we also have stories of water and fire fighting for power. Also we are told that there was a fight between water and wind, and water is said to have won. *Awasüng* and *arisüng*, two kinds of trees, too fought. Now the *arisüng* sent its roots down deep underneath the ground. While they were fighting, the *arisüng* cut off the branches and the leaves of *awasüng*. However, the roots of *awasüng* tree occupied a larger area which made it firm and strong so finally *arisüng* lost to him.

Tekatia Imchen: True, there are so many stories about the competition of power amongst different elements like the stories about fire and water, sun and storms. But we should see these as simple elements competing to know who was more powerful than the other, and not as gods.

Student: There are many gods who are all under the one Supreme God who is the lord of the universe. This could be a safe description.

Arenjenba Ozukum: As a matter of fact, our Ao ancestors addressed different gods as Yimkong Tsüngrem (God of all), Ita-anü Tsüngrem (moon-sun god) and Lijaba Tsüngrem (creator of the earth).

Teacher: The tradition variously uses terms like Teyanglur, Jongpotemtem and Teroktsünger to describe Tulutiba, the greatest God.

Rongsenwati Longchar: In earlier times, people were laughed at by the church people if they worshipped trees but today they worship statues and sacred buildings and also call upon the church pastor and church members asking them to sanctify even their brand new vehicles! Our ancestors worshipped Asüngalong Tsüngrem (tree and stone gods) because they provided them their daily necessities. The Hindus too take a holy bath in Ganges River. Our ancestors worshipped their gods with *auk* (pig), *an* (hen) and *entsükhang* (egg basket) because *temenen* told them to worship him by offering the right kind of sacrifices in order to get divine blessings.

Merazulu Longchar: Let me say this in another way. In the church, we don't worship the buildings or the materials used for buildings but we worship the Holy Spirit in order to attain salvation. We never worship the vehicle but we pray to our Lord to have his blessings upon us as we use the vehicle for our earthly purpose.

Similarly in olden days, we worshipped the stones and trees because we believed that there was some kind of divine force in them.

Visitor: Dear sirs you describe the autonomy and supremacy of various gods but you also say that god is one.

Temsula Ao: This is wrong. There is not any one god. There are only different gods.

Guru Sademmeren Longkumer: Yes there are many gods and each of them possesses different powers. Let me explain. For our forefathers all the forces that surrounded them were gods. We were told by them that Lijaba made the earth, Lord of the sky rules the sky, and human beings and the animals have burst out from Teroktsünger god. We have Longtitsüngba and also Meyutsungba who is believed to be the god of ultimate judgement. We also have Awatsüng Tsüngrem (god of lake), Tenem Tsüngrem (god of mountain), Kimong Tsüngrem (homestead god), Alu Tsüngrem (field god) and we have many more. We were also told that Osaknü Tsüngrem is the fiercest god of all.

Student: This point is clear but the question of one god residing in many, whose majesty flows through all, remains unclear.

Meyawati Walling: Let us put it simply. There is only one God but he appears in different forms.

Tareptsüba: Different names are used in addressing god, but there is only one god.

Bendangangshi: It may be thought that traditional Ao religion is polytheistic because of the belief in the plurality of gods. Although, the tradition speaks of so many gods, they believed really only in one god called Teroktsünger (greatest god). All the names mentioned above are nicknames of Teroktsünger god. So powerful and great was Teroktsünger god, people never mentioned his name when they worshipped him. They addressed him as Ita-anü Tsüngrem (moon-sun god), Anüngtsüngba (god of the sky) instead. God of the sky and moon-sun god are the metaphorical expressions for Teroktsünger. It is believed that Teroktsünger lives in the land of the sun where there are thousands of palaces. He is served by one of the *tenyar* (angels) called *zonichilar*. There are three kinds of *tenyar*: (i) *kodak tenyar*, (ii) *tsüngrolar*, and (iii) *zonichilar* (one who makes home on the sun). When he opens his palace door to send out *zonichilar* as messenger to different parts of the world, the sound of his palace door can be heard only by the cocks; that is why when the cocks crow, human beings know the arrival of the dawn. It is said beautiful girls are compared to *zonichilar*. Teroktsünger is also called Sobatiyaba (god of destiny) because of the belief that human beings came to this world through him and it is he who makes their fate and destiny. Teroktsünger is the greatest god among all the gods mentioned.

Korakaba Jamir: Allow me to put all that we have said briefly. There are three important gods in the traditional Ao belief system. Lijaba Tsüngrem who created the earth, Meyutsungba (god of judgement) who judged the souls in his courtyard and

Anüngtsüngba the god of sky. They believed only in one god but worshipped the god in different manners by giving different names. Lijaba, Meyutsungba and Anüngtsüngba are believed to be one god.

Ita-anü Tsüngrem was never worshipped but mentioned in all the rites and rituals. During different seasons, all the rituals and sacrifices were performed in order to invoke blessings from god. Yimkong Tsüngrem was the god of all and Awatsüng Tsüngrem was worshipped because he saved the villagers from their enemies.

XIV

Of God and the New Religion

Visitor: Respected elders by your admission, there has been a drastic change in the sacred geography of the Aos. In such a scenario what happens to the ancient gods?

Guru Sademmeren Longkumer: In olden days, we worshipped the big rocks and trees because we believed that there was god residing there. But now we can never accept such a conception as we have outlined earlier. Christian doctrine teaches us that our ancient religion is sinful. So, we have followed Christian teachings and discarded our ancient religion.

Kikasangla Imchen: I believe all gods are equal. There is only one God and all gods are one. With this understanding in me, I did not embrace the new religion which is known as Christianity. My late parents had converted to Christianity but I did not. I followed the Ao religion while they were still alive, and continued to do so after their conversion. If I go to school, then I will be asked to accept the Christianity (*dhurom*) that is why I decided not to go to school.

Visitor: Do the ancient gods live in spite of Christianity or are they all gone?

Guru Sademmeren Longkumer: No doubt, the ancient gods are still there but we were told by the Christian missionaries to confess the sins we have committed by worshipping the ancient gods. So, we leave the ancient religion and convert to Christianity. However, if we do bad things or insult the ancient gods then havoc will befall upon us even now.

Teacher: After they have converted to Christianity, they discarded the ancient religion because worshipping of ancient gods was taught to be sinful by the Christian missionaries but they know and believe that those forces or gods are still there in the world. The presence of those forces or gods is still believed and talked about even to this day. And if we go to a haunted place even now, we feel the presence of some force in that area.

Student: One of our elders a non-believer (non-Christian) told me that his god is still there. He makes his presence felt wherever he goes.

Visitor: Most of the knowledgeable persons present in our midst belong to a generation, that has experienced a life centred around the presence of the ancient gods but the question arises in connection with their grandchildren, will the gods still be there for them or not?

Merazulu Longchar: Till the end of the world everyone will believe in the presence of the ancient gods.

Student: It is the Christian doctrine that has taught them that all the ancient gods are evil, so as Christians they have to repeat that.

Tekatia Imchen: Otherwise the church will not accept them. Whosoever recognizes them as gods, their names will not be enrolled as members in the church.

Student: But they know in their heart whatever ancient gods that Aos have worshipped those gods with all their force will remain the same. This will be passed from one generation to another even though they have abandoned the earlier belief system.

Teacher: But you are not getting the whole picture. Don't you see the environment which housed the different gods has been already degraded? Trees have already been cut down, sacred rocks are destroyed, so what of the sacred habitat?

Guru Sademmeren Longkumer: Even if we have converted to Christianity, big stones, trees and forests are left untouched because they fear that those forces are still there.

Merazulu Longchar: We don't worship them now but they are still preserved.

Meyawati Walling: Time will tell what kind of an environment the youngsters will live in. The younger generation will deal with whatever situation presents itself to them. How we were before and how we are now is very different; things have undergone a lot of change. Therefore, we can't say much about the future at this point.

Student: May I ask our elder from Longkhum how does she view the present in relation to her village after the advent of Christianity? Which world is better, the world of her forefather's time or the world after conversion to Christianity?

Kikasangla Imchen: Our ancestors lived a simple and truthful life. From my experience, I have known that our forefathers had a prosperous life, the old religion and life were better than the contemporary times. This is the reason why I am not converting and joining the Christian religion.

Teacher: Respected Shri Meyawati, can you tell me your reason for not converting to Christianity?

Meyawati Walling: Let us make one thing clear. We do not wish to either praise our goodness or insult other religions in not converting to Christianity. There are so many religions in the world yet we do not wish to pick and choose we wish to remain truthful and that we can do only in our own religion that is where we find our happiness. We vowed to remain truthful therefore we decided not to convert to any other religion. We have already grown old so we won't be able to contribute anything by changing to the new religion. We want to be happy in life for that it is not necessary to convert into another religion. We are not telling that Christianity is bad and our religion is good. It is our understanding and belief that if we are truthful to our god, he will bless us. No matter, how much we talk about issues related to religion, our ultimate aim and need is only god. Therefore, we should praise him and live a truthful life.

Of course, other people's thinking and interest are different. Some people switch from one religion to another, let them do so if they think that they will find their happiness in doing that. We can neither stop them nor direct them in what they should do. Our understanding is to find happiness in what we do and believe. If we are truthful in our speech and act, we find happiness. Therefore, we have decided to remain in the same religion we were born in and have not converted to Christianity.

We now talk about Jesus Christ but prior to his coming, there was also God. God created the earth so we should praise and obey him. We should live a truthful life for that is what he wants from us. God searches only our hearts. We accept both the blame and praise from the people who judge us. Our goal is to live a truthful and happy life. We teach our children to live a truthful life and to give their best service to the people and not to bring any shame on us. We tell our children not to feel ashamed of thinking that their parents are 'animists'. We tell them to go to church regularly.

Student: We Christians believe that our god is the real god. Can you really prove to yourselves that the god you believe in is the real one?

Meyawati Walling: We are not claiming that our god is the real and true god and your god is unreal and untrue. Whatever people think of us let them think. They tell us that our god is not the true and real god, that we believe in *temenen* (evil) god. But there is only one god. What is the difference between *temenen* god and not *temenen* god? They won't be able to explain and differentiate the two. We offer our rituals to the Teyanglur Tsüngrem (creator god) only and not to *mojing* or *temenen tsüngrem*. People may talk so many things but over and above all and the most important one is the god who creates us.

Student: Let us ask Shri Meyawati also this question. As you have personally witnessed both the traditional and the new worlds what do you think about the situation now? Which of the two worlds is a better place to live in?

Visitor: But we have been told about a fight between the water god and the fire god competing for power.

Meyawati Walling and Yabangchila Imchen: Both water and fire were regarded as most important by our ancestors because the water sweeps away everything without leaving anything and the fire burns up everything into ashes. We were told that no other elements can compete with them. There was a fight between fire and water and water is said to have won the fight.

Longrimongba Mongru: Yes we also have stories of water and fire fighting for power. Also we are told that there was a fight between water and wind, and water is said to have won. *Awasüng* and *arisüng*, two kinds of trees, too fought. Now the *arisüng* sent its roots down deep underneath the ground. While they were fighting, the *arisüng* cut off the branches and the leaves of *awasüng*. However, the roots of *awasüng* tree occupied a larger area which made it firm and strong so finally *arisüng* lost to him.

Tekatia Imchen: True, there are so many stories about the competition of power amongst different elements like the stories about fire and water, sun and storms. But we should see these as simple elements competing to know who was more powerful than the other, and not as gods.

Student: There are many gods who are all under the one Supreme God who is the lord of the universe. This could be a safe description.

Arenjenba Ozukum: As a matter of fact, our Ao ancestors addressed different gods as Yimkong Tsüngrem (God of all), Ita-anü Tsüngrem (moon-sun god) and Lijaba Tsüngrem (creator of the earth).

Teacher: The tradition variously uses terms like Teyanglur, Jongpotemtem and Teroktsünger to describe Tulutiba, the greatest God.

Rongsenwati Longchar: In earlier times, people were laughed at by the church people if they worshipped trees but today they worship statues and sacred buildings and also call upon the church pastor and church members asking them to sanctify even their brand new vehicles! Our ancestors worshipped Asüngalong Tsüngrem (tree and stone gods) because they provided them their daily necessities. The Hindus too take a holy bath in Ganges River. Our ancestors worshipped their gods with *auk* (pig), *an* (hen) and *entsükhang* (egg basket) because *temenen* told them to worship him by offering the right kind of sacrifices in order to get divine blessings.

Merazulu Longchar: Let me say this in another way. In the church, we don't worship the buildings or the materials used for buildings but we worship the Holy Spirit in order to attain salvation. We never worship the vehicle but we pray to our Lord to have his blessings upon us as we use the vehicle for our earthly purpose.

Similarly in olden days, we worshipped the stones and trees because we believed that there was some kind of divine force in them.

Visitor: Dear sirs you describe the autonomy and supremacy of various gods but you also say that god is one.

Temsula Ao: This is wrong. There is not any one god. There are only different gods.

Guru Sademmeren Longkumer: Yes there are many gods and each of them possesses different powers. Let me explain. For our forefathers all the forces that surrounded them were gods. We were told by them that Lijaba made the earth, Lord of the sky rules the sky, and human beings and the animals have burst out from Teroktsünger god. We have Longtitsüngba and also Meyutsungba who is believed to be the god of ultimate judgement. We also have Awatsüng Tsüngrem (god of lake), Tenem Tsüngrem (god of mountain), Kimong Tsüngrem (homestead god), Alu Tsüngrem (field god) and we have many more. We were also told that Osaknü Tsüngrem is the fiercest god of all.

Student: This point is clear but the question of one god residing in many, whose majesty flows through all, remains unclear.

Meyawati Walling: Let us put it simply. There is only one God but he appears in different forms.

Tareptsüba: Different names are used in addressing god, but there is only one god.

Bendangangshi: It may be thought that traditional Ao religion is polytheistic because of the belief in the plurality of gods. Although, the tradition speaks of so many gods, they believed really only in one god called Teroktsünger (greatest god). All the names mentioned above are nicknames of Teroktsünger god. So powerful and great was Teroktsünger god, people never mentioned his name when they worshipped him. They addressed him as Ita-anü Tsüngrem (moon-sun god), Anüngtsüngba (god of the sky) instead. God of the sky and moon-sun god are the metaphorical expressions for Teroktsünger. It is believed that Teroktsünger lives in the land of the sun where there are thousands of palaces. He is served by one of the *tenyar* (angels) called *zonichilar*. There are three kinds of *tenyar*: (i) *kodak tenyar*, (ii) *tsüngrolar*, and (iii) *zonichilar* (one who makes home on the sun). When he opens his palace door to send out *zonichilar* as messenger to different parts of the world, the sound of his palace door can be heard only by the cocks; that is why when the cocks crow, human beings know the arrival of the dawn. It is said beautiful girls are compared to *zonichilar*. Teroktsünger is also called Sobatiyaba (god of destiny) because of the belief that human beings came to this world through him and it is he who makes their fate and destiny. Teroktsünger is the greatest god among all the gods mentioned.

Korakaba Jamir: Allow me to put all that we have said briefly. There are three important gods in the traditional Ao belief system. Lijaba Tsüngrem who created the earth, Meyutsungba (god of judgement) who judged the souls in his courtyard and

Anüngtsüngba the god of sky. They believed only in one god but worshipped the god in different manners by giving different names. Lijaba, Meyutsungba and Anüngtsüngba are believed to be one god.

Ita-anü Tsüngrem was never worshipped but mentioned in all the rites and rituals. During different seasons, all the rituals and sacrifices were performed in order to invoke blessings from god. Yimkong Tsüngrem was the god of all and Awatsüng Tsüngrem was worshipped because he saved the villagers from their enemies.

7. Ita-anü Tsüngrem (Moon-Sun)

XIV

Of God and the New Religion

Visitor: Respected elders by your admission, there has been a drastic change in the sacred geography of the Aos. In such a scenario what happens to the ancient gods?

Guru Sademmeren Longkumer: In olden days, we worshipped the big rocks and trees because we believed that there was god residing there. But now we can never accept such a conception as we have outlined earlier. Christian doctrine teaches us that our ancient religion is sinful. So, we have followed Christian teachings and discarded our ancient religion.

Kikasangla Imchen: I believe all gods are equal. There is only one God and all gods are one. With this understanding in me, I did not embrace the new religion which is known as Christianity. My late parents had converted to Christianity but I did not. I followed the Ao religion while they were still alive, and continued to do so after their conversion. If I go to school, then I will be asked to accept the Christianity (*dhurom*) that is why I decided not to go to school.

Visitor: Do the ancient gods live in spite of Christianity or are they all gone?

Guru Sademmeren Longkumer: No doubt, the ancient gods are still there but we were told by the Christian missionaries to confess the sins we have committed by worshipping the ancient gods. So, we leave the ancient religion and convert to Christianity. However, if we do bad things or insult the ancient gods then havoc will befall upon us even now.

Teacher: After they have converted to Christianity, they discarded the ancient religion because worshipping of ancient gods was taught to be sinful by the Christian missionaries but they know and believe that those forces or gods are still there in the world. The presence of those forces or gods is still believed and talked about even to this day. And if we go to a haunted place even now, we feel the presence of some force in that area.

Student: One of our elders a non-believer (non-Christian) told me that his god is still there. He makes his presence felt wherever he goes.

Visitor: Most of the knowledgeable persons present in our midst belong to a generation, that has experienced a life centred around the presence of the ancient gods but the question arises in connection with their grandchildren, will the gods still be there for them or not?

Merazulu Longchar: Till the end of the world everyone will believe in the presence of the ancient gods.

Student: It is the Christian doctrine that has taught them that all the ancient gods are evil, so as Christians they have to repeat that.

Tekatia Imchen: Otherwise the church will not accept them. Whosoever recognizes them as gods, their names will not be enrolled as members in the church.

Student: But they know in their heart whatever ancient gods that Aos have worshipped those gods with all their force will remain the same. This will be passed from one generation to another even though they have abandoned the earlier belief system.

Teacher: But you are not getting the whole picture. Don't you see the environment which housed the different gods has been already degraded? Trees have already been cut down, sacred rocks are destroyed, so what of the sacred habitat?

Guru Sademmeren Longkumer: Even if we have converted to Christianity, big stones, trees and forests are left untouched because they fear that those forces are still there.

Merazulu Longchar: We don't worship them now but they are still preserved.

Meyawati Walling: Time will tell what kind of an environment the youngsters will live in. The younger generation will deal with whatever situation presents itself to them. How we were before and how we are now is very different; things have undergone a lot of change. Therefore, we can't say much about the future at this point.

Student: May I ask our elder from Longkhum how does she view the present in relation to her village after the advent of Christianity? Which world is better, the world of her forefather's time or the world after conversion to Christianity?

Kikasangla Imchen: Our ancestors lived a simple and truthful life. From my experience, I have known that our forefathers had a prosperous life, the old religion and life were better than the contemporary times. This is the reason why I am not converting and joining the Christian religion.

Teacher: Respected Shri Meyawati, can you tell me your reason for not converting to Christianity?

Meyawati Walling: Let us make one thing clear. We do not wish to either praise our goodness or insult other religions in not converting to Christianity. There are so many religions in the world yet we do not wish to pick and choose we wish to remain truthful and that we can do only in our own religion that is where we find our happiness. We vowed to remain truthful therefore we decided not to convert to any other religion. We have already grown old so we won't be able to contribute anything by changing to the new religion. We want to be happy in life for that it is not necessary to convert into another religion. We are not telling that Christianity is bad and our religion is good. It is our understanding and belief that if we are truthful to our god, he will bless us. No matter, how much we talk about issues related to religion, our ultimate aim and need is only god. Therefore, we should praise him and live a truthful life.

Of course, other people's thinking and interest are different. Some people switch from one religion to another, let them do so if they think that they will find their happiness in doing that. We can neither stop them nor direct them in what they should do. Our understanding is to find happiness in what we do and believe. If we are truthful in our speech and act, we find happiness. Therefore, we have decided to remain in the same religion we were born in and have not converted to Christianity.

We now talk about Jesus Christ but prior to his coming, there was also God. God created the earth so we should praise and obey him. We should live a truthful life for that is what he wants from us. God searches only our hearts. We accept both the blame and praise from the people who judge us. Our goal is to live a truthful and happy life. We teach our children to live a truthful life and to give their best service to the people and not to bring any shame on us. We tell our children not to feel ashamed of thinking that their parents are 'animists'. We tell them to go to church regularly.

Student: We Christians believe that our god is the real god. Can you really prove to yourselves that the god you believe in is the real one?

Meyawati Walling: We are not claiming that our god is the real and true god and your god is unreal and untrue. Whatever people think of us let them think. They tell us that our god is not the true and real god, that we believe in *temenen* (evil) god. But there is only one god. What is the difference between *temenen* god and not *temenen* god? They won't be able to explain and differentiate the two. We offer our rituals to the Teyanglur Tsüngrem (creator god) only and not to *mojing* or *temenen tsüngrem*. People may talk so many things but over and above all and the most important one is the god who creates us.

Student: Let us ask Shri Meyawati also this question. As you have personally witnessed both the traditional and the new worlds what do you think about the situation now? Which of the two worlds is a better place to live in?

Meyawati Walling: There is a wide gap between these two worlds. In olden days, people were truthful and hard-working. If they worked hard, they earned enough for their survival and if they could not, they endured the pain of hunger. Today, in this world, we can get money only through untruthful means. No one speaks the truth now, whatever they do, building houses and acquiring material goods; they do so by using money earned by untruthful means. People do not want to do agricultural work so they try to earn money for their survival by telling lies. We want to tell you that in today's world there is no one who speaks the truth.

Yabangchila Imchen: There is indeed a wide gap between these two worlds. Our ancestors' wealth was generated by their hard work and through truthful means. However, in today's world without telling lies, one docs not earn anything.

Glossary

achangki/asangki	a thatched house made of fern at the outskirt of the village
ak	pig
akimeyimlawa	name of a herb most commonly used in rituals in olden days
ali	land
alu	paddy field
amou	is a ritual observed by the Ao ancestors (*genna*). The day they observed *amou*, the entire villagers would stay at home without going anywhere
amongsangemer	widower
amtsarong	cluster of banana trees
amwa	banana leaves
anpong	egg basket
ansülong	name of a stone god found in Süngratsü village
antepong	cock
Anüngtsüngba/ Longtitsüngba Tsüngrem	god of the skies
anüm	an instrument used for weaving by the Ao womenfolk
anümeyi	full moon

anüngnoza	refers to women/females
anü	sun
aonglemla	a creature resembling a woman found in deep jungle
aotetsü-tebou	Ao ancestors
arapu	cane bridge
aratsütep	tug-of-war
ar	cane
arju	dormitory for men
arjukima	compound in a dormitory
arong	dyed hair used for decoration in the Ao traditional attire
arsalang	cane platform
asürmongzü	hawks of the dead people
asüyimdong	street in the land of the dead
atakror	invoke
athi/jen	granary
au	bamboo
azük	necklace
awatsüng Tsügrem	god of lake
awayabu/ausou	plate made of bamboo
azü	dog
azüngketer	one who possesses extraordinary power
balaluyuba	divorce
bendanger	strangers
bhokbo	owl
changchangwa	name of a local herb
chapeli	it is equivalent to money which was used in olden days

charmelok	village local tax
Chungli	a dialect in Ao language
chunglier	people who speak Chungli dialect
Chungliyimti	the first Ao settlement
demen	road
diphulima/diphuyim	land of the dead
entsü	egg
entsükang	egg basket
fokorep	shreds of clay pot
fovong	old clay pot
idangeter	village spies
ilangtsür	clan-women
ita	moon
Ita-anü Tsüngrem	moon-sun God
itaerem	month end
jakranglongpang	up hill
jangpetwa	name of a scented herb
jeshi	bamboo jar
ketachir	bastards
khüling	seeds of the sword-bean creeper
kidong	clan
kimem	to be physically clean
kimak	courtesy visit
Kini Tsüngrem	homestead god
kitsüngmong	worship of house
konangnüngsang	honour
kumpang	ivory armlet
lakep	sea shell

lazasübo	name of a cliff beyond the Wokha hills
lenden	plain
lendangsangji	street bastards
Lijaba	creator of the earth
Lijabamong	worship of Lijaba
longritsü	stream of bitterness towards the land of the dead
longsüputu	golden period
Longtitsüngba	God of the sky
Long Tsüngrem	stone god
longterok	literally six stones
Lumong Tsüngrem	field god
masü	cow
meimchir	human beings
melar	widow
mepu	colony/sector
merüaao	a group of people who were left behind by the gone ones (Aos) after the cane bridge was cut off
moatsü/moatsümong	worship of Lijaba and also the biggest and most important festival of the Aos
mojing	devil/evil
Mongsen	a dialect in Ao language
Mongsener	people who speak the Mongsen dialect
monguzenojang	a variety of fig fruit
mongzü	hawk
mongzüki	cave of the hawks
Motsüngba/ Meyutsungba	God of justice

Mosakni Tsüngrem	God of the lake. This god was believed to be the fiercest god
mürütsü	name of an ant
nabakvo	a variety of bean family
alimayimyayimpu	nature
nisungsangla	referred to human beings in olden days and was considered to be the eldest among all the living creatures.
nokinketer	warrior
nokleptsü	waist belt worn by the Ao men
nokpang	dao-holder
nü	spear
ochi	truth
ochishir	one who speaks the truth
ong	chief councillor
onger	a person who hold the post of the chief councillor in the village council
ongputu	name of an epoch
pakti	mat
porep	clay pot
putir/patir	a retired person who was a member in the village council in any epochs
rongmi	an ornamented spear made of bamboo
rongsen	property/possession
samen	the actual enforcer of all the rules and regulations of the village in Mongsen village council
sangmonger/sangmore/ arasentsür/Ratsünlar	soothsayer. She was a mediator between the dead and the living. She

	was consulted for finding out the cause of one's illness and of its cure
sangremer	widower
sangtemsangtema	who went freely
sangtemer	refers to a group of people, an existing tribe in Nagaland
sarasadem	prayer
Sartiyong	name of a river found in Süngratsü village in Ao territory
semtu	rest camp
senmang	inheritance
senmanger	a person who inherits the ancestral property
shipu / saretpha	boar tusk necklace
shiruru	animals
shirung	fox
sobaliba	culture
Sobatiyaba Tsüngrem	god of destiny
sü	*mithun*
süachiba	feast of merit
sülieawoer	trance
süngdonglidong	plants and trees
sünglang	sit-out platform attached to the main building in a traditional Ao house
süngtidong	it is a tree standing tall at Meyutsungba's courtyard. Every soul has to pierce the tree. Men used *nü* (spear) and women used *anüm* (a tool used for weaving). those who hit the mark were proved to be truthful and those who miss the mark

	were proved to be untruthful ones
tanüla	soul/spirit
tatar	headman
tazüng	the actual enforcer of all the rules and regulations of the village in Chungli village council
tekolok	brain
Tekong Tsüngrem	mountain God
tekülem	worship
temang	body
temeim	love
temenen	evil
temra	veranda attached to the main building at the backyard of a house
tenem	mountain
Teroktsünger	according to one version Teroktsünger was believed to be the Supreme God in the traditional Ao belief system
Teyanglur Tsüngrem	creator god
tinu	best friend
tiptsüngdi	side wall
tongpang	warfare
tongshi	pillar post
tsükchir	enemy
Tsülayong	name of a river in Ao territory
tsüleplu/lepluarsangla	sea beetle
tsüngrem	god
tsüta	marshy lake
tsütayongpang	marshy shoreline at the edge of a river

tsüngkum	season
tsüngremmong	worship of Lijaba and also the second major festival of the Aos
tsünü	wolf
tsüngzü	offering
tsumalima	refer to the plains of Assam
tongpang	war
walunir	a capable leader and also a person who give feast to the villagers by killing *mithun*s
yaren	luck
yimden	political institution
Yimkong Tsüngrem	god of all
yimli	the entitlement that belongs to a particular clan in the village/gracious
yimpangmejongben	magpie bird
Yimrong	a place where they lay the trophy heads brought to the village
yimrongkülemba	worship of Yimrong
yimsüsür	administrator
yimtsüng	village
yongmen	brass ring
Yongpang Tsüngrem	river god

Appendix

List of Ao elders who participated in the discussion

Sl. No.	*Name*	*Village*	*Age (yrs)*	*Occupation*
1.	Tekatia Imchen	Longkhum	88	farmer
2.	Meyawati	Longkhum	82	farmer
3.	Pangchenmeren	Longkhum	86	farmer
4.	Longdangsüja Mongru	Longkhum	90	farmer
5.	Bendangangshi	Ungma	79	Theologian
6.	Tareptsüpa	Longkhum	88	farmer
7.	Guru Sademmeren Longkumer	Ungma	82	Retd. school teacher
8.	Arsashi Jamir	Süngratsü	75	farmer
9.	Rongsenwati Longchar	Yimyu	89	Retd. school teacher
10.	Longrimongba Mongru	Longkhum	89	farmer
11.	Arenjenba Ozukum	Mopungchukit	70	farmer
12.	Nungshimangyang Longchar	Süngratsü	86	farmer
13.	Ariyongdang Longchar	Khensa	92	farmer
14.	Sashimeren Walling	Khensa	80	Retd. school teacher
15.	Repjensangba Longchar	Süngratsü	90	farmer

16.	Bendangsashi Longchar	Süngratsü	85	farmer
17.	Korakaba Jamir	Mopungchukit	77	farmer
18.	Satiba Jamir	Mopungchukit	92	farmer
19.	Merazulu Longchar	Süngratsü	84	farmer
20.	Ms Kikasangla Imchen	Longkhum	86	farmer
21.	Meyawati Walling	Longkhum	85	farmer
22.	Ms Yabangchila Imchen	Longkhum	80	farmer
23.	P. Ato. Jamir	Khar	76	Ex. Gaon Borah
24.	Imtinochet Jamir	Khar	76	Ex. Gaon Borah
25.	Tako Jamir	Chuchuyimlang	58	Computer Technical Assistant, Public Work Department

DK PRINTWORLD